"Susan Albers has written a superb manual for teenagers that provides expert information and advice about food, mood, and mindful eating. This book offers creative and engaging ways for teens and any to truly understand mindful eating to learn about this important subject, but more importantly, to take action to feel more at ease with food and their bodies."

—**Carolyn Coker Ross, MD, MPH**, speaker, pioneer in the use of integrative medicine for eating disorders and addictions, and author of *The Emotional Eating Workbook*

"Susan Albers's new book, *Eating Mindfully for Teens*, is the perfect solution to navigating emotional eating challenges in teens. I love the scripts that she provides, the active journal exercises, and her suggestions for movement and other healthier solutions for when teens need more energy, or to calm their emotions. I will absolutely share this with my teen daughter, my clients, and the mothers in my practice."

—**Jessica Drummond, DCN, CNS, PT, NBC-HWC**, founder and CEO of The Integrative Women's Health Institute

"I was thrilled to receive an advanced copy of Susan Albers's new book, because I knew she had included a section on sleep (activity eight) where she correctly identifies the effect of sleep on mindful eating. In addition, she gives great activities for teens—known to be incredibly sleep deprived—to participate in. This will be a great resource for anyone working with teens and mindful eating."

—**Michael Breus, PhD**, The Sleep Doctor™

"The teen years can be challenging in so many ways, including struggles with body image, relationships, and emotions. Susan Albers's workbook practically tackles the unhealthy relationships teens can develop with food, and provides a much-needed resource in this area. I highly recommend it for parents and professionals looking to teach teens the tools for making a lifetime of healthy choices around food, while improving self-image, resilience, and coping skills in the process."

—**Nicole Beurkens, PhD, CNS**, licensed psychologist and certified nutrition specialist

"*Eating Mindfully for Teens* is an invaluable resource for both parents and practitioners to help children create beneficial eating habits that last a lifetime. Inside are practical strategies to avoid overeating and make healthier food choices, without fad dieting. Susan Albers is a pioneer and leads the mindful eating revolution."

—**Joe Tatta, DPT, CNS**, bestselling author of *Heal Your Pain Now*

"It's so encouraging to read a book that teaches a wise and rational approach to eating instead of another quick-fix or temporary diet. Susan Albers's *Eating Mindfully for Teens* offers the effective technique of mindfulness as a method to help teens develop a healthy relationship with food that they can put into place and hopefully keep for the rest of their lives."

—**Lisa M. Schab, LCSW**, adolescent psychotherapist specializing in disordered eating and anxiety; and author of *The Anxiety Workbook for Teens, The Self-Esteem Workbook for Teens,* and *Beyond the Blues*

eating mindfully
for teens

a workbook to help you make healthy choices, end emotional eating & feel great

SUSAN ALBERS, PsyD

Instant Help Books
An Imprint of New Harbinger Publications, Inc.

Publisher's Note

This publication is designed to provide accurate and authoritative information in regard to the subject matter covered. It is sold with the understanding that the publisher is not engaged in rendering psychological, financial, legal, or other professional services. If expert assistance or counseling is needed, the services of a competent professional should be sought.

Distributed in Canada by Raincoast Books

Copyright © 2018 by Susan Albers
      Instant Help Books
      An imprint of New Harbinger Publications, Inc.
      5674 Shattuck Avenue
      Oakland, CA 94609
      www.newharbinger.com

Cover design by Amy Shoup

Acquired by Tesilya Hanauer

Library of Congress Cataloging-in-Publication Data

Names: Albers, Susan, author.

Title: Eating mindfully for teens : a workbook to help you make healthy choices, end emotional eating, and feel great / Susan Albers, PsyD.

Description: Oakland, CA : New Harbinger Publications, Inc., [2018] | Audience: Age 14-18.

Identifiers: LCCN 2017045786 (print) | LCCN 2017047173 (ebook) | ISBN 9781684030040 (PDF e-book) | ISBN 9781684030057 (ePub) | ISBN 9781684030033 (paperback)

Subjects: LCSH: Teenagers--Nutrition--Psychological aspects--Juvenile literature. | Teenagers--Nutrition--Psychological aspects--Popular works.

Classification: LCC RJ235 (ebook) | LCC RJ235 .A43 2018 (print) | DDC 613.20835--dc23

LC record available at https://lccn.loc.gov/2017045786

20   19   18

10   9   8   7   6   5   4   3   2   1   First Printing

To Brooklyn and Jack, my favorite mindful eaters

For teens and readers:

Visit http://www.eatingmindfully.com/teens to download three videos on easy, fun ways to manage stress and feeling overwhelmed!

For parents and health care professionals:

Visit http://www.eatingmindfully.com/helpers for a must-see video on the three best strategies to encourage teens to eat more mindfully!

Contents

Section One: Mindful Eating

Section Two: Mood

Section Three: Mindset

Section Four: Motivation

Dear reader,

Thank you for reading *Eating Mindfully for Teens.*

You are taking your first step in an exciting journey to eating in a brand new way—one that makes you feel energized and happy about your food choices and shows you how to enjoy food in a healthy way.

Well-meaning adults in your life—health teachers, PE teachers, caregivers, parents, or friends—may have talked with you about healthy eating. Or perhaps you have read articles on social media about the healthiest foods or have seen online ads that promise you instant results: "Slim down in ten days with this one weird trick!" This book takes a slightly different approach. First of all, I don't tell you *what* to eat. I don't say, "don't eat sugar" or "eat more vegetables." Instead, we will discuss *how* to eat: how to make food decisions—like choosing a healthy food versus junk food—and when to start and stop eating. It also tackles a lot of the other questions that go along with eating, such as how to make healthy choices when your friends are not and how to feel better on a stressful day.

Second, this book isn't something you sit down and silently read. It's an interactive guide that helps you learn how to stay healthy, manage your weight, feel good about your body, and feel energized. Consider this workbook to be a body-positive tool you can use as often as you need to help you stay on track and focused when it comes to being the healthiest version of yourself.

This workbook covers four topics—*mindful eating, mindset, mood,* and *motivation.* These four things will help you to take charge of your eating habits right now! You should know that in this workbook, you will see the term *mindfulness* often. Mindfulness is your key to having a new relationship with food. Basically, mindfulness is being more present and aware of your experience as it happens. In this workbook, the focus is on being present and aware of your style of eating and your interactions with food. It's easy to eat mindlessly—out of routine, habit, or just to get it over with. A mindful approach to eating dives deeper into the *what, how,* and *why* you are eating so that you make choices you really want to make. Food decisions don't have to be stressful, difficult, or fearful. They can be fun, healthy, and some of the most important decisions you make all day.

Once you begin using this workbook, you will never look at eating the same way again. Best of all, I will help you gain confidence, self-esteem, and a sense of control over your life that you may have never thought possible.

Are you ready to get started?

Let's dive in!

Mindfully yours,

Susan

P.S.: If you have a parent or health professional you are working with, please loan them this workbook and have them read the letter on the next page, which I have written to them.

letter to parents and clinicians

Dear parents and clinicians,

Thank you for purchasing this workbook for your teen or client. It's never too early to learn mindful eating skills. *Eating Mindfully for Teens* will show young adults how to deal with important day-to-day challenges with food—from the choices they make right now to long-term habits they develop for years to come. This workbook will walk teens through how to avoid overeating and how to make healthier food choices without fad dieting. The practical activities in the workbook discuss topics such as navigating school lunches, making better food choices, and feeling good about your body. The skills are based on the clinically proven principles of mindful eating.

If you work with teens in counseling or are a parent of one, this is a must-have workbook. It will give them a solid foundation for eating well in high school and college. You can't always be with your child to guide his or her food choices. And it's not easy for teens to feel good about their bodies, given the body-obsessed media that bombard them, or make smart food choices in our current world, which is filled with fast food and highly processed foods. Why not give them solid tools for making healthy decisions on their own? I've seen a lot when it comes to teens! I am a psychologist who has been working at one of the top five health care institutions for over a decade. I also am the author of eight books on mindful eating. In my office, I see teens every day who struggle with their body image and how to eat. I also meet with men and women who wish they had started learning how to eat better earlier in their lives. So I have learned a lot about the real struggles teens encounter every day. I am also a parent myself—I have a boy (in grade school) and a girl (a teenager). We've been working on mindful eating skills from day one. Thus, I care deeply about these issues not just on a professional level but on a personal one as well.

I recently met with a mother who had been trying to get her teen to improve her eating habits for months. Every day after school, her daughter snacked mindlessly in front of the television and then refused to eat a healthy dinner. Her daughter was defensive and constantly rolled her eyes at her mother whenever she tried to talk to her about her food choices. It wasn't working. The frustrated and exhausted mom stopped trying to give advice. Instead, she got some of the handouts I've created for teens and left them in her daughter's room without a word. Within days, she noticed her daughter beginning to make more conscious choices rather than rummaging mindlessly through the kitchen! This mom loved the approach so much that she signed herself and her daughter up for my online program, which they could access from their phones, which you can see on http://www.eatingmindfully.com.

I've seen mindful eating work with my clients firsthand, but this workbook is based on much more than just anecdotal evidence from my own practice. Over the past ten years, there has been a growing body of research on mindful eating. A recent review of twenty-one papers using mindfulness-based interventions to address binge eating, emotional eating, external eating, and dietary intake found that 86 percent of the reviewed studies reported improvements in eating behaviors.[1] Wow! This is great news!

If you are a health care practitioner or caregiver, this workbook can give you some concrete tools to use with teens. Please consider sharing this workbook with your clients. They will obtain the most value from working through each activity themselves. There are assignments and journal activities that you can give as you work together to learn these concepts.

Again, thank you for helping your teen or client establish a healthy relationship with food! And please feel free to go to my website, http://www.eatingmindfully.com, to learn more about how mindful eating can be helpful for adults too! I have many free tools that show you how to be an amazing role model.

Mindfully yours,

Susan Albers, PsyD

---

1   O'Reilly, G. A., L. Cook, D. Spruijt-Metz, and D. S. Black. 2014. "Mindfulness-Based Interventions for Obesity-Related Eating Behaviours: A Literature Review." *Obesity Reviews* 15(6): 453–61.

what is mindfulness?

The first thing you might be wondering is, *What exactly is mindfulness?* Simply put, mindfulness is active awareness. It's the ability to live *in the moment*, without distracting thoughts or judgments about the past or future. Basically, it is focusing on what is happening right now.

Too many people live their lives in a rush, racing from one activity to the next—without ever taking the time to focus on the here and now. For instance, let's say your mom is driving you to soccer practice. Instead of enjoying the view out the window, feeling the cool rush from the air conditioner on your skin, and really listening to the song on the radio, you're busy worrying about tomorrow's precalculus exam, wondering if the upcoming team will beat you, and feeling bad about a fight you had with your boyfriend at lunch. *That* is the opposite of mindfulness, yet so many people live their lives in this anxious, hurried state, so distracted by their thoughts that they don't really experience what they are doing. The danger of zoning out is that you do things without thinking or enjoying them.

On the other hand, when you're mindful, you focus your attention in a nonjudgmental way on the current moment—right here, right now. Mindfulness is your ability to concentrate on the present moment *only*. Being mindful allows you to focus on the now, no matter what you're doing: studying, finishing chores, eating, or hanging out with friends.

To give you a better sense of how to experience mindfulness, try the following experiment. Take a deep breath, in through your nose and out through your mouth. Look up from this book and notice what you see around you. Choose at least five items to focus your attention on. For example, if you're sitting cross-legged on your bed in your room, you might look up from your book and see your lamp, your chair, your phone, your laptop, and your cat. You let your eyes drift over each item and identify each one in your head. Think to yourself:

I'm looking at the lamp. The lamp has a white base and a pink shade.

(Pause.)

I'm looking at my chair. It's a black desk chair that swivels.

(Pause.)

I'm looking at my phone. The case is cracked. There's a long jagged line going down the back.

As you do this, notice how your breathing slows and how vivid the items you've selected suddenly seem. This is mindfulness! It is complete and total awareness of an object, person, or feeling. For one moment, it's the only thing that exists in your mind. In fact, you may begin to notice things about the object you had never paid attention to before while practicing mindfulness.

My black desk chair has a small hole in the bottom. I never noticed that before. I wonder if the cat did it. Or: *I've never really looked up at the sky. The clouds are amazing. I'm usually just running off to class, looking straight ahead, thinking about my homework.*

Basically, mindfulness could have the motto, "Right here, right now."

Now, you may be wondering how mindfulness applies to eating. Typically, people get into distinct patterns when it comes to eating—they get stuck in a rut. You can eat an entire plate of food and not taste one bite. You may be used to scarfing down your food as quickly as possible while checking social media or binge watching your favorite show. It may seem strange to you at first to slow down and be aware of eating. Being mindful while eating, however, allows you to experience food and eating on a much deeper, more satisfying level.

what is mindful eating versus mindless eating versus dieting?

Let's take a look at the differences between these three things.

Mindless Eating: Mindless eating is eating out of habit and zoning out while doing it. Eating popcorn at a movie theater is a good example. Sometimes you aren't even really tasting it, and by the time you realize what's going on, you've lost touch with how much you've eaten.

Dieting: Dieting often includes restricting or cutting out some foods (like carbs) while eating more of other kinds of foods (like meat or vegetables) and sometimes limiting yourself to certain food combinations. It can involve extreme portion control, calorie counting, and even feeling like you're starving yourself. No matter what you hear or read, fad dieting is *not* a healthy way to manage your weight. Why? We need all foods in healthy balance to get a wide range of nutrients.

Mindful Eating: Mindful eating is balancing *how* you eat with *what* you eat. Mindful eating is not a diet, and there are no menus or recipes. It's about being fully aware when you're eating. This means noticing the amount of food you're eating, its taste and texture, and it means truly enjoying your food. As a result, you slow down and recognize when you are full. This gives you a feeling of being in charge of how much you're eating. This is making conscious rather than habitual food choices.

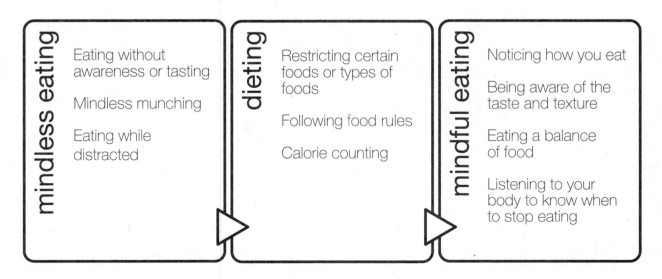

mindless eating

Eating without awareness or tasting

Mindless munching

Eating while distracted

dieting

Restricting certain foods or types of foods

Following food rules

Calorie counting

mindful eating

Noticing how you eat

Being aware of the taste and texture

Eating a balance of food

Listening to your body to know when to stop eating

Figure 1. **Mindless Eating Versus Dieting Versus Mindful Eating**

Believe it or not, zoning out is very common. The constant flood of information via texting, social media, videos, and news clips can simply overwhelm your brain. Whether you realize it or not, when you slip into the behavior of mindless eating (or mindless walking and texting, mindless biking, or mindless driving), that's your poor brain trying to take a break! When you eat mindfully, not only will you be giving your brain a rest by focusing on one thing at a time, but you'll also actually be able to enjoy your food!

the benefits of mindful eating

There are many reasons to practice mindful eating.

Reason 1: There's no fad dieting involved. One of the best things about mindful eating is there's no dieting involved. No restrictions, no calorie counting, no measuring, and no guilt. When you're not dieting, you can't slip up—no matter what you eat! You can enjoy *all* foods.

Reason 2: It's not scary. Every day you get a lot of information online, from magazines, and from parents and friends telling you what to eat, what not to eat, and how often to eat it. A lot of it is conflicting and confusing. This can make you anxious about food in general, and it also can make you feel insecure about your body. Mindful eating is not scary. There are no strict rules, and you can move at a pace that is comfortable for you.

Reason 3: It's kind. Mindful eating focuses on self-acceptance and encourages you to treat yourself with compassion. It helps you learn not to be hard on yourself or to call yourself names.

Reason 4: It makes you feel good about your body. Here's a secret: mindful eating will teach you how to feel good about your body *right now*, which will keep you on the path to treating your body with care.

Reason 5: The mindful eating activities are totally easy to do. With mindful eating, you only focus on what you would normally eat every day. That's it! There are no confusing instructions, and you don't have to add yet another activity to your already busy life.

Reason 6: It's a whole-body approach. Mindful eating focuses on all aspects of your experience with food (mind, body, thoughts, and feelings). That means that it taps into whatever is standing in the way.

Reason 7: Literally everybody can do it. Whether you're in middle school, high school, or college; male or female; a mindless eater, overeater, undereater, or chaotic dieter—it doesn't matter. Absolutely *everyone* can use mindful eating—and that includes *you*!

Reason 8: It works. Scientific research has shown that mindful eating helps you to take charge of your eating habits.

Reason 9: It lasts. Because you are learning to be more in charge of your eating habits, mindful eating is an excellent long-term way to eat.

Now you're probably asking, *What's the catch?*

Good question.

Here's the answer: there is no catch. I'll prove it. Go ahead and put this book down. Find your absolute favorite food in the world. Whether it's a slice of pizza, a piece of chocolate cake, a candy bar—it doesn't matter. Just go grab it.

Got your favorite food? Great.

Here's what you do:

Look at it. Let's say it's a piece of candy. Don't pop it into your mouth just yet. First, look at the shape of the candy. Is it round? Square? What color is it? Is its surface shiny or dull? Then notice how it feels in your hand—the weight of it. What else do you notice about it? Take a few seconds to really look closely at the candy (or whatever it is you're eating).

Smell it. Bring the piece of candy up to your nose and give it a tentative sniff. Savor its aroma. Take a longer sniff of it. Feel your mouth watering in anticipation of the tasty treat. Do this for at least fifteen seconds.

Taste it. Now take one small bite and chew slowly—don't gobble it or swallow it whole (which you may feel like doing at this point). Allow the flavors to burst onto your tongue. Notice the taste and the texture.

Chew it. You might think, *Chew now? Wait. I've been chewing!* Yes, I know. I put chewing here as a separate step because many people don't even finish the food in their mouths before taking a second or even a third bite. This is why I recommend chewing the first morsel carefully before taking another bite.

Swallow it. When you've finished chewing, slowly allow the bite to slide down your throat. (You're laughing now, aren't you?)

Now, enjoy the rest of your candy, repeating the steps outlined above.

While breaking down the process of eating one small piece of candy may seem a bit ridiculous, it has a purpose. Eventually, you will be able to do this automatically, without thinking through the steps, and it won't seem weird at all.

By completing this exercise, you've just experienced a little "taste" of mindful eating.

A key part of mindful eating is being nonjudgmental. You will hear this over and over again in this book. I realize that this is not easy—but it's the cornerstone of mindful eating. In other words, you will learn how to respond when you mind gets critical about your food choices. The mind is often flooded with negative thoughts about your actions: *How could you be so dumb—why did you just eat that?* or *No, no, no—you shouldn't be eating that!* As you begin to eat mindfully, you will learn to quiet those criticisms.

How did your first experiment with mindful eating feel to you? Was it different than other eating experiences you have had?

_____

_____

_____

Hopefully, you noticed a few things. Perhaps being tuned in and slowing down helped you to enjoy the experience more and also to be more aware of the entire experience.

how to find additional resources

If you feel you've lost control over your eating, are fearful of eating, or have any other anxieties or frustrations around food, your weight, or your body, it is important to talk with your parent, guardian, physician, therapist, or guidance counselor. You may need more support if

- you feel out of control,

- you feel ashamed or guilty,

- you feel stuck,

- you are experiencing physical problems as a result of your eating,

- you have an eating disorder or other serious eating concerns,

- you feel depressed or anxious,

- you have thought about harming yourself, or

- you can't seem to put mindful eating into practice after you've finished reading this book.

Before consulting a trusted adult, write down what concerns you the most. Share the list with that person or simply say, "I'm concerned about my eating habits. Can you help me?"

_____

_____

_____

_____

Please be cautious when searching the Internet for information or guidance. Some websites are helpful, while others can be harmful, with misinformation or unhealthy advice. It is better to ask a trusted professional for helpful resources.

Let me introduce myself. My name is Dr. Susan Albers, and I have been a psychologist for over fifteen years. As the author of eight books, I've helped thousands of people eat more mindfully. During this time, I've worked at four colleges, and I currently have a private practice where I see many high school and college students (and those who can't come to my office, I see online).

Not only that, but when I was younger, I experienced what many teens today face: a lack of reliable, healthy information and advice about eating and food. During my high school years, I received no education on healthy eating—no nutrition classes or instructions whatsoever. Until I went to college, I just ate what my parents fed me with little to no thought. I wasn't alone. One friend would buy mint cookies from the lunch line and dip them in a chocolate milkshake. Talk about a sugar bomb each afternoon! Other friends stuck to the same food for six months straight—pizza!

I distinctly remember walking into the massive dining hall at the College of Wooster the first day and feeling overwhelmed by the number of options: the salad bar, hot line, vegetarian line, cold sandwiches, and the dessert bar. I had no strategy and no idea where to begin. Thankfully, over the years, I've learned a lot. I reflect back to that time and wish I had been armed with some tools on that very first day.

Many of my former clients return during or after college to thank me for the tools I gave them—tools you'll find in this workbook and in my other books. I appreciate knowing that the strategies made a difference. These clients realized how valuable it is to know *how* to eat, especially once they were on their own, making their own decisions.

In addition to introducing myself, I'd like to introduce you to some people you will meet in this book. They are based on real people I know and have worked with in my office. This will give you an indication of the type of teens I work with on a daily basis. (Disclaimer: All names and distinguishing characteristics are changed to protect the individuals' privacy.)

Take a look at the list below, and think about which of them you identify with the most.

- Stacie, age 14: Always dieting, like her mom.

- Rachel, age 17: Feels out of control. Sometimes overeats, and other times does not eat very much. Exercises to "get rid" of calories but doesn't really enjoy it.

- Theresa, age 18: Eats healthy but hates her body and feels bad about specific parts of her body, like her stomach and legs.

- Jayden, age 19: Has body issues, dislikes how he looks, and feels insecure. Is not confident and usually "feels fat."

- Marco, age 15: Has body issues and feels like he doesn't have muscles. Worries that other people don't find his body attractive.

- Emma, age 16: Feels pressured to look like her sister and friends.

- Chloe, age 15: Is a picky eater who only eats junk and eats mindlessly.

- Thalia, age 18: Is a stress eater and eats when bored.

If one or more of these people sound familiar to you, this book will address your feelings and will help you put an end to your unhealthy relationship with food.

Mindful Eating

Mindful eating is a way of helping you make decisions about what is just the right amount of food for you—no one else. Unfortunately, there are no rules and no one-size-fits-all answer about what to eat and what not to eat—though diet books would like to convince you otherwise! In reality, it's all about knowing what your body needs and being able to honor it. The good news is that mindful eating is a way of helping you get to know your hunger from the inside out.

1 how to get started being more mindful today

Theresa: *My first semester in college was so overwhelming; I couldn't focus on anything. I thought I was going to flunk out. When I started practicing mindfulness and focused on only one thing at a time, not only did my grades improve, but my friends noticed a positive change in me, too. I made better decisions about everything—from the boys I dated to the food I ate.*

for you to know

When you are mindful, you are 100 percent focused on the lecture you're listening to, the friend you're talking with, or the food you're eating—without allowing other thoughts to get in the way. But this doesn't mean that other thoughts won't sometimes pop up. Our brains are busy little bees that buzz off in every possible direction. If you find your attention wandering from whatever you're doing (and it will), just gently return your focus back to the moment. Listen to the sound of your breath. Notice the pace of your heart beating.

for you to do

Here are some other ways you can practice mindfulness over the next few days.

Listen to a Friend.

Stephen Covey, author of *The Seven Habits of Highly Effective People*, once said, "Most people do not listen with the intent to understand; they listen with the intent to reply." It's true. Have you ever had a conversation with your friends, but you weren't really listening to what they were saying? Your brain was so busy coming up with a response that you missed something important—and your response was so out of context that there was an uncomfortable silence? If this has happened to you, don't worry! It's extremely common. But there's a good way to avoid the awkwardness and have more meaningful interactions with your friends. Simply practice mindfulness during conversations. Here's what you do:

- Stop what you're doing—put your phone or homework aside.

- Pay attention to your friend's words closely. Look her in the eyes.

- Notice her facial expressions.

- Listen to the tone of her voice.

- Notice her body language. Is she folding her arms across her chest, or is her foot fidgeting around?

You'll be amazed at how many things you pick up when you start being mindful. You'll realize how much you missed before. And one great side benefit of introducing mindfulness into your relationships is that you'll be teaching by example. Eventually, the people around you will start doing the same thing and will be more mindful of you.

Mindfully Watch a Television Show, Movie, or Video.

You already watch videos, movies, and shows, so why not do so mindfully?

- Choose a show you've never seen before.

- Listen to the characters as they speak to each other.

- Pay attention to their body language as they interact.

- Focus on the main plot of the show.

(Note: The reason you should pick a show you haven't seen before is that if you're too familiar with it, you'll be more tempted to multitask—texting, doing homework, or checking your social media accounts.) While you're watching the show, resist the urge to do anything else and just fully focus on it. This is mindful behavior.

Take a Mindful Bath.

Baths are so relaxing. The next time you take one, try this:

- Leave your book, cell phone, or other distractions in your bedroom.

- Draw yourself a warm bath, watching the water as it flows from the faucet.

- Sink into the water, noticing how it feels on your skin.

- Lie back, close your eyes, and just pay attention to the feeling of being in the water.

- You can try moving your hands through the water to feel its pressure, or sink a bit lower and let your hair float out behind you.

Just be there in that moment. If your mind wanders, simply bring your attention back to the feel of the water on your skin. This practice can be done in a shower as well—paying attention to the water hitting you, flowing down your face and body, and so forth.

more to do

When beginning the practice of mindfulness, it is helpful to keep a journal. This way, you can keep track of each mindful behavior you engage in each day. This gives you something to look back on (another way to be mindful!) to note your progress. This workbook can serve as your journal. When you have some quiet time, consider the prompts below, and answer them. For example, perhaps it was easy to be mindful when talking with a friend, and your mind wandered most when you were sitting in class.

- Today, I was most mindful or present when…

- Today, I was least mindful when…

- Tomorrow, I am going to work on being more mindful when…

_____

_____

_____

_____

_____

_____

Technology is often one of the biggest obstacles to mindfulness. Take this challenge: Put your phone or technology away while you're with a friend. Don't even have it with you. Journal about your experience. Did this change the way you interacted?

2 the secret to enjoying food—without guilt

Chloe: *I've always been a really picky eater. My mom says I would turn my nose up in disgust at most foods when I was little. For about a year, I lived on chicken nuggets and grape juice. I wouldn't eat anything else. We went to a dietitian who suggested mindful eating, and I thought it was weird. But I've been doing it for a few months now, and I'm starting to eat foods I didn't even want to look at before.*

for you to know

Mindful eating is just like mindful listening, mindfully watching a show, or bathing mindfully. It's the same principle, only applied to food. When you eat mindfully, you slow down and enjoy your food—really tasting it, instead of just shoveling it down to make the hunger pangs, stress, or boredom go away. And if you're anxious about what you eat, mindful eating helps remove the worry and guilt. You stop judging your food and eating. Instead, you simply observe and notice what you're eating—without criticism or scolding.

for you to do
Practice Mindful Eating.

For this activity, choose a few bites of food—something that includes pieces. It could be small pieces of candy, pretzels, cereal, or small chunks of fruit. Put five pieces of your chosen food into a small bowl, and put the rest away so you won't struggle with wanting more. (Note: It's important to try this activity when you're not really hungry. Once you learn more about mindful eating, you'll be more tuned in to your body and less likely to feel that type of hunger. But for this exercise, you should be just slightly hungry—not ravenous.)

I've talked a lot about the "Five S's of Mindful Eating" in other books that I've written, and these tips may help you stay on track during your mindful eating experiments:

1. *Sit.* Sit down and focus all your attention on eating. No cell phones, computers, or other distractions.

2. *Slow.* Proceed slowly and carefully. This helps you notice and fully appreciate the act of tasting your food and pacing yourself. Really look at the small pieces of food in front of you. Notice their shape, texture, and scent. Put the first piece of food in your mouth and chew slowly.

3. *Savor.* Notice the flavors and texture of the food. This helps you enjoy the process of eating. In your mind, make a list to help you stay tuned in to what you're eating: *sweet, chewy, fruity, dark chocolate, a hint of coconut.*

4. *Swallow.* Swallow the first piece of food before picking up another piece.

5. *Smile.* After you've swallowed each bite, smile. Smiling releases positive emotions that make you less likely to want to overeat. The pause also gives you a moment to decide if you want more or not.

Repeat the same process with the other four pieces. Then, describe the experience of eating mindfully. Was it frustrating, fun, interesting, or boring? Here are some prompts to get you started:

- When I tried mindful eating today, I found it to be…

- The most important thing I learned from mindful eating today was…

- Tomorrow, I will remember to continue my practice of mindful eating by…

_____

_____

_____

_____

_____

_____

more to do

Now it's time to set some goals. Set at least three goals to eat more mindfully. As you brainstorm, remember that I am not talking about weight loss goals. These should be about the process and habits of mindful eating. For example:

- Tomorrow, when I eat dessert, I'm going to slow down and savor every bite.

- This week, I'm going to pay closer attention to the flavors of the foods I eat.

- I'm going to buy my favorite soda at the market on the way home from school. But instead of chugging it as I walk, I'm going to wait until I get home. I will pour the soda into a glass, sit down, drink it slowly, and actually enjoy it.

_____

_____

_____

_____

_____

journal exercise

Now choose one of the goals above and journal about how it impacted you.

- My goal was…

- The goal was _____ (hard, easy, etc.) to complete because…

- To keep this goal going, I would need to…

_____

_____

_____

_____

_____

_____

breaking mindless eating habits 3

Emma: *I eat exactly the same lunch every single day. It's just my habit. I get frustrated when I don't have my usual things to eat and have to buy the school lunch. But nothing is going to change if I don't try something new.*

for you to know

There are many reasons people overeat or get into unhealthy situations with food—even when they don't mean to. For some, mindless eating is a habit that they aren't even aware of. The following activity will help you identify any food routines, rituals, or habits that may be keeping you stuck. Keep in mind that it is normal to have habits and routines. Some routines are helpful, because you don't have to give them much thought and they are healthy—like brushing your teeth. Others routines make your mind dull—especially when you just go along with the flow without making active and conscious choices. Becoming aware of your habits can turn it all around.

for you to do
Quiz: Do I Eat Mindfully?

You may be wondering, *Do I eat mindfully?* If you aren't sure, this quiz on your mindful eating skills will help you identify which skills you may want to boost. As you take this quiz, remember to notice what you already do well. Keep in mind, there are no right or wrong answers, so be honest!

1. I tend to stop eating when I am full.

All of the time   Most of the time   Sometimes   Occasionally   Almost Never

2. I eat when I'm physically hungry, rather than when I'm emotional.

All of the time   Most of the time   Sometimes   Occasionally   Almost Never

3. I try not to pick at food or eat it just because it is there.

All of the time   Most of the time   Sometimes   Occasionally   Almost Never

4. I savor each bite of food before reaching for the next.

All of the time   Most of the time   Sometimes   Occasionally   Almost Never

5. When I eat, I think about how I'm nourishing my body.

All of the time   Most of the time   Sometimes   Occasionally   Almost Never

6. I do not judge myself, my body, or the times when I overeat.

All of the time   Most of the time   Sometimes   Occasionally   Almost Never

7. I don't multitask when I eat; I just eat.

All of the time   Most of the time   Sometimes   Occasionally   Almost Never

8. I don't have to eat everything on my plate. I can leave what I don't want or what I'm not hungry for.

All of the time   Most of the time   Sometimes   Occasionally   Almost Never

9. I tend to eat slowly, chewing each bite.

All of the time   Most of the time   Sometimes   Occasionally   Almost Never

10. I recognize when I slip into mindless eating (zoning out, popping food into my mouth).

All of the time   Most of the time   Sometimes   Occasionally   Almost Never

Each statement in this quiz describes an aspect of mindful eating. As you review your responses, are there any statements you want to work on? For example, maybe you need to be more tuned in to when you feel hungry and full so you don't overeat. Or perhaps you notice that you're always telling yourself to eat more slowly. Or maybe you simply want to be more present and aware as you eat.

Take a moment and list one or two mindful eating goals for yourself. If you're stuck, check out these sample goals to get you started:

- *To chew my food completely so that I eat more slowly.*

- *To ask myself after each bite if I'm still hungry or if I'm full.*

- *To notice the texture and taste of each bite—to be more aware of my food.*

_____

_____

_____

_____

more to do

So you may have noticed from the quiz that sometimes mindless eating is just about habits—repeating a regular practice or behavior without much thought, like brushing your teeth or combing your hair. Here is your opportunity to examine closely what habits might be keeping you stuck and to reset them. Choose one of the habits listed below to target this week. At this point, all you have to do is be mindful of it—examine it. For example, if you eat while watching television, make sure to pay attention to this habit. Notice if there are any patterns to it. Every day? At night? When you're bored? You will find that when you start to pay attention to habits, just noticing them sometimes prompts you to do them a little differently.

Eating Habits

_____   I like to eat at the same time no matter what.

_____   I eat food just because it is there.

_____   I eat at scheduled times whether I am hungry or not.

_____   I bring the same foods to school every day without thinking about it.

_____   I eat during my favorite television shows, whether I am hungry or not.

_____   I eat in the same places or restaurants on a particular day of the week.

_____   I feel bad or frustrated if I can't have my usual snack.

_____   I get annoyed if a restaurant doesn't have my favorite food.

_____   I buy the same foods each time I go to the grocery store.

_____   I sit in the same seat or place every day when I eat.

Now choose one habit (and an antidote to that habit) and focus on it for one week. Use the chart below to keep track of your progress. For example, you could have the habit of eating while watching television. An antidote could be eating only at the kitchen table.

Habit and Antidote	Mon	Tues	Wed	Thurs	Fri	Sat	Sun

journal exercise

Now it's time to reflect on what you learned about your food habits.

- A habit I have that leads to mindless eating is…

- I can replace that habit with a healthy, mindful habit like…

- What might stand in the way of changing this habit?

_____

_____

_____

_____

_____

_____

putting the brakes on speed eating 4

Marco: *I've always been a fast eater, and having three older brothers makes it worse. If you don't eat your share—and eat it quickly—you go without. Even when I'm out with friends or just chilling in my room, I still eat like somebody is going to snatch it away from me. Sometimes I eat so fast that I get a stomachache.*

for you to know

You live in a much faster-paced world than your parents ever imagined. There's so much to do, see, and focus on that it's hard to notice your own body's needs. Whether you're a fast eater because you're anxious that you won't get enough food, like Marco, or you just want to get eating out of the way so you can do more important things, you can learn to slow down.

Slowing down when you eat has many health benefits. It keeps your blood sugar levels balanced to help prevent sugar cravings, and it keeps you from overeating until you feel sick. Eating slowly also helps you to feel fuller and recognize when it's time to stop eating. Most important, when you chew slower, you enjoy food more, and it gives your body time to digest what you've eaten.

for you to do

Focusing on chewing more slowly helps you avoid eating too much and regretting it later. Here are six ways you can begin to slow down:

- *Set your intention.* Before you start eating, tell yourself, *I'm going to slow down for this meal.* Setting an intention helps you to focus more closely on eating mindfully.

- *Notice others.* The next time you're in the school cafeteria or out for a bite with friends, notice how fast they eat. Some people eat slowly, while others scarf down the whole meal in one bite. Others are somewhere in between.

- *Cut your food into smaller pieces.* When it comes to eating, fast eaters are likely not only to eat quickly but also to take gigantic bites. But if you're taking huge bites and eating too quickly, you're also probably not chewing your food well. This means almost-whole pieces of food are ending up in your gut, and then it's up to your poor stomach to do the work that should have started in your mouth. This can lead to stomachaches, heartburn, poor digestion, nausea, and unexpected weight gain. If you have this tendency, you're not alone, and one way to break this habit is to cut your food into smaller, more manageable bites.

- *Chew for twenty seconds.* Once you have a smaller bite of food in your mouth, chew it slowly for at least twenty seconds before swallowing. Did you know that it takes twenty minutes for your brain to receive a message from your stomach and realize that you've had enough to eat? That means that, if you've eaten two servings of food in ten minutes but you still feel hungry, it's because your brain hasn't gotten the message yet. This also explains why you feel sick later on.

- *Create a mindful pause.* Between bites, take a mindful pause. Some examples of mindful pauses are:

  * taking a breath
  * taking a drink
  * switching utensils
  * putting your fork down for a moment

- *A counting exercise.* Try this when you're alone. Run your finger around the edge of the circle and count the number of chews it takes to completely break down the bite.

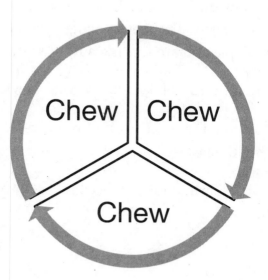

Figure 2. A Counting Exercise

Now choose one of the methods above to help you slow down while you eat. For one week, commit to trying it out. Write about your experience.

- How challenging was it to eat more slowly, on a scale from 1 to 10 (10 being the most challenging), and why?

_____

_____

_____

- How did slowing down impact how much and what you chose to eat?

_____

_____

_____

more to do

Try this challenge! Notice how quickly your friends and family eat. We tend to automatically eat at the same rate without even being aware of it. For one week, actively eat more slowly than the people you are sharing a meal with.

1. When you sit down, mindfully take a pause and see who starts eating first.

2. Look around the table and rate, on a scale from 1 to 10, how quickly people are eating, with 10 being the fastest.

3. Now try eating at your normal rate. Notice how it compares with the people you're eating with.

journal exercise

Once you've done the challenge for a week, journal about your experience.

- Were you able to eat more slowly than all of your friends and family?

- How would you describe your pace? Slow as a turtle or quick as a jackrabbit?

- What did you notice about the way that different people in your life eat? Whose eating patterns best mirror yours? And whose are the most different? Why?

_____

_____

_____

_____

_____

_____

5 how to not turn into a raisin

Chloe: *Not only am I still pretty much a picky eater, but I also hate the taste of water. I learned in school that my body is about 60 percent water, but when there's fruit juice and soda around, why would anyone drink just plain water? I was shocked when my dietitian told me I was dehydrated all the time and that soda drains you of water. Dehydration can make me moody and make my muscles cramp up. No wonder I feel so tired and cranky!*

for you to know

When it comes to choosing what to drink, water is almost always the best option. It does amazing things for your body. Sipping water each day helps to regulate your metabolism, digest your food, and even make food taste better. Water also helps your skin and gives you energy to do everything you need to. Every cell in your body needs water to function well.

Not drinking enough water can affect your ability to concentrate and can make you feel tired, anxious, and irritable. It can also make you think you're hungry—when you're actually just thirsty. When you keep yourself hydrated, you will naturally have more energy, without the need for a caffeine pick-me-up. But you should avoid soda and energy drinks (and even juice). The problem with those drinks is that they contain lots of sugar and caffeine, which actually draws water out of your body. Dehydration makes it hard to focus, robs you of energy, and makes you feel bad all the way around.

for you to do

Let's set a challenge for this week. Aim for at least four eight-ounce glasses of water a day. You don't have to do it all at once. Each day of the week, plan to increase your water intake by four ounces (half a cup). By the end of the week, you will be up to 32 ounces per day. Track your daily water consumption listed in the chart below.

Mon	Tues	Wed	Thurs	Fri	Sat	Sun
8 oz. 9 a.m.	8 oz. 10 a.m.	8 oz. 9 a.m.	8 oz. 9 a.m.	8 oz. 9 a.m.	8 oz. 9 a.m.	8 oz. 9 a.m.
	4 oz. 2 p.m.	4 oz. 2 p.m.	4 oz. 2 p.m.	8 oz. 2 p.m.	8 oz. 11 a.m.	8 oz. 11 a.m.
		4 oz. 9 p.m.	4 oz. 6 p.m.	4 oz. 6 p.m.	4 oz. 2 p.m.	4 oz. 12 p.m.
			4 oz. 9 p.m.	4 oz. 9 p.m.	4 oz. 6 p.m.	4 oz. 2 p.m.
					4 oz. 9 p.m.	4 oz. 6 p.m.
						4 oz. 9 p.m.

Helpful Hints to Meet the Challenge

- *Set a specific goal.* Know where you are now. Start there and increase by half a cup at a time or whatever you can manageably do. Knowing what you're aiming for can help. If you tend to forget, you can get an app for your phone that will remind you.

- *Set deadlines and reminders.* Set three alarms to remind you to take a drink! Or set a deadline (*I will drink a glass of water by 10 a.m.*).

- *Connect it with another routine already in place.* You brush your teeth twice a day without any thinking or effort, so drink a glass of water after you brush them. Easy!

- *Eat foods higher in water content.* Foods like cucumbers, grapes, popsicles, salad greens, grapefruit, cantaloupe, and watermelon are all high in water content.

- *Beware of thirst vampires.* There are foods and drinks that suck the hydration right out of you! Coffee, soda, salt, and energy drinks will undo all your efforts.

more to do

The Water Bottle Challenge

The best way to increase your water intake is to make sure it is handy and convenient. Your challenge this week is to find a fun water bottle (BPA free) and carry it with you wherever you go. Feel free to decorate it or personalize it to make it your own.

journal exercise

Write down your water goals below.

_____

_____

After a few days of working on these goals, reflect on your progress.

- Today, the most difficult thing about keeping my body hydrated was…

- Today, I switched out _____ sugary drinks with water.

- Tomorrow, my goal is to replace _____ more nonwater drinks with water.

- I drank _____ glasses of water today, and I felt…

_____

_____

_____

_____

6 figuring out just the right amount to eat

Rachel: *It seems like I eat a lot less than my family. I don't have second helpings, like my brother. But when I look at my friends, it seems like I eat more than they do. I am confused about what is the right amount to eat and whether I am overeating or undereating. How can I know how much I should be eating?*

for you to know

How much is the "right" amount to eat can be confusing, because there is no hard and fast guideline that applies to everyone. How much you should eat depends on many factors, including your activity level, whether you are male or female, and your height, age, muscle composition, and genetics. What's key is that you start being aware of how different portion sizes impact your energy level, level of satisfaction, and mood. Sometimes we only need one bite to feel satisfied, and other times we need a large bowl or full plate to feel content.

for you to do

Today, be mindful of your portion sizes.

1. Before you fill your plate, think about how much you are taking. Visually judge the size of your portions. Ask yourself, is the portion size of your food the size of:

   - your thumb,

   - the length of your ring finger,

   - your fist,

   - the entire flat surface of your hand, or

   - the inside cup of your hand?

2. Then, evaluate how the portion makes your body feel (satisfied? still hungry?) and how it impacts your mood (regretful? guilty? proud of holding back from another portion?).

   - When I have thumb-sized amount of peanut butter on my toast, I feel...

_____

_____

_____

_____

3. If you want a challenge, play with your portion sizes. Increase or decrease the size by just a bite and see what happens. Or commit to trying a different portion size listed above.

more to do

Something that dramatically influences how much you eat is the plate or bowl in front of you. This week, your challenge is to use a different plate or utensil. Try one of these things:

- Use a salad plate instead of a dinner plate (bigger plates lead people to eat bigger portions).

- Use a small spoon instead of a large spoon.

- Use a tall, narrow glass (which creates the illusion that it holds more) instead of a small, wide glass.

- Use a different color plate. Scientific studies say we eat the most when we use white plates and the least with red (when your brain sees the color red, it automatically thinks *Stop!*).

- Try putting a snack in a small bowl instead of a larger bowl (and always remember to avoid eating right from the bag).

journal exercise

Write about what you noticed in your experiments with your portion sizes and your mood.

- When did you tend to be the most mindful of portion sizes? (When you were trying a new food, eating a dessert, or sharing?)

- When were you the least mindful of how much you were eating? (When you were sitting in front of the television, were alone, or when someone served you food?)

- What did you learn from being mindful of portion size?

- Which portion size do you tend to prefer, and how does it feel when you eat too much or too little?

_____

_____

_____

_____

_____

_____

_____

7 how hungry am I?

Rachel: *I could eat all the time. But then I get overly full and feel awful—bloated and uncomfortable. Sometimes I just inhale my food. After I finish a bowl of chips, I think to myself, "I didn't even really enjoy that at all! They were gone before I even realized what I was doing."*

for you to know

It's important to understand that *feeling hungry is normal and healthy*. Your body needs fuel to function. You can and should learn to understand and be mindful of your hunger. When you know exactly how hungry you are, you can respond appropriately to your body's cues for food with just the right amount or portion size—just a bite or a full meal.

for you to do

Before you even take a bite, ask yourself, *How hungry am I on a scale from 1 to 10?*

1. Overly hungry, starving, dizzy, weak

2. Pretty hungry, stomach growling a lot, very hungry

3. Noticeably hungry, beginning to feel out of energy, stomach starting to rumble

4. Starting to want something to eat, thinking about food

5. Satisfied, not hungry or full

6. Full, content, pleasant

7. A little bit beyond full, starting to feel uncomfortable

8. Stuffed, uncomfortably full

9. Stomach feeling very full, feeling significant discomfort

10. Extremely full, feeling sick

more to do

Now that you have been tuning in to your hunger, try tracking the patterns in your hunger level for one week. For example, when you get up, identify how hungry you are on the scale, and write it down. This will help you to choose the amount to eat for breakfast—a big breakfast or maybe just a smoothie.

	Mon	Tues	Wed	Thurs	Fri	Sat	Sun
Waking Up							
Mid-Morning							
Noon							
Afternoon							
Evening							
Before Bed							

journal exercise

Write about your experience with tracking your hunger.

- I notice that I am the hungriest when…

- The part of the day I am the least hungry is…

- I need to pay attention most to my hunger when…

_____

_____

_____

_____

_____

_____

8 how to manage your appetite while you sleep

Thalia: *I heard in health class that teenagers need a lot of sleep, but by my junior year of high school, that just wasn't happening. I had way too much to do. I was taking all AP classes, so I had a ton of homework. I was on the softball team, and I had just gotten my first part-time job. I was lucky if I slept five hours a night! That's when I noticed the weight gain. Because of all the stress, all I did was eat. It was my way of coping, I guess.*

for you to know

Did you know that people around age thirteen to eighteen need approximately nine hours of sleep each night to function at their best? Most teenagers only get about seven. Much of this has to do with early school start times, extracurricular activities, lots of homework, part-time work, and social obligations. In college, it can be even tougher to get that much-needed rest. There are so many fun and interesting things to do that sleep may be the last thing on your mind. You may feel like you don't have time to sleep!

You may be thinking, *What does sleep have to do with eating mindfully?* Well, when you're tired, you might have more cravings and be more likely to overeat or binge on food—both of which are efforts to feel more awake when what you really need is sleep. In part, this happens because less sleep messes up the hormones that regulate your normal appetite by signaling that you are hungry or full. Also, when you are tired, you don't make the best decisions about anything—including food. You're more likely to think, *Oh, whatever,* and reach for a bag of chips.

for you to do

First, familiarize yourself with some of the top tips. In the left-hand column of the chart below, make a check mark next to the tips that you feel might help you to get more sleep.

✓	Sleep Sabotages	Try These! Sleep Helpers
	Caffeinated drinks: these rev up your system.	Chamomile or herbal tea, tart cherry juice (helps raise melatonin levels), or warm milk.
	Sugary snacks: sugar gives your blood glucose a sudden increase that, some say, can wake you up.	Foods with tryptophan (a chemical that helps to put you to sleep): hummus and veggies, parmesan cheese popcorn, oatmeal, bananas, yogurt, turkey, cheese, or nuts.
	Screen time: the blue light of phones has been shown to interfere with melatonin, the hormone that helps you sleep.	Turn off the sound and lay the phone facedown or at least three feet from your head.
	Television: television doesn't help you to unwind your brain. You can get caught up in the story line and engaged mentally.	Journal, play some music. Unwind!
	Naps: a long nap in the afternoon can make you sleep poorly that night.	Naps can help you catch up on your sleep, but nap for no more than thirty minutes.
	An irregular bedtime: going to bed at ten one night and two in the morning the next.	Make a pretty firm bedtime to help you unwind. Do the same steps each night in the same order. Your brain loves consistency. If you go to bed at the same time every night, you will train your body to begin to fall asleep.
	Poor sleep conditions: a room too hot or too cold (or a messy environment) can harm your sleep.	Keep your room a cool 60 to 67 degrees, but put on warm socks, which has been shown to help people sleep. And clean up your room. Make a Zen space to sleep, with soft blankets and clean sheets.

Next, try this: For the next week, commit to addressing at least one of the sleep sabotages above and try one of the sleep helpers. See if this helps you to sleep and even out your appetite. Remember: a well-rested brain = better decisions.

more to do

If you're someone who has trouble falling asleep, try the following tips:

- A yoga technique called "left nostril breathing" is known to reduce your blood pressure and calm you down. Lie on your left side. Rest your finger on your right nostril and gently close it. Slowly breathe in through your left nostril. Place your thumb on your left nostril and close it as you exhale from your right nostril. Repeat as many times as needed.

- While lying down, try rolling your eyes up several times. This is the action that your body naturally does as it falls asleep, so it tricks your mind into falling asleep.

- Try humming. Close your mouth. Breathe in deeply, then breathe out gently, creating a humming vibration. The gentle vibrations can help calm the body. Give your body some suggestions as well as you do this. Think to yourself, *I am about to fall asleep* or *My body is relaxing*.

- If you're worried about something, get up and jot down your thoughts. This will help you to let them go, at least for the evening.

_____

_____

_____

_____

journal exercise

In the space below, write about your experiences.

- My biggest obstacles to getting a good nights sleep are _____

_____

- When I go to bed earlier, I feel _____

_____

- Write down five of your normal activities that you would be willing to reduce. For example, you could record your favorite show one night a week instead of staying up late to watch it, or you could attend a group meeting every other week instead of weekly. Talk with your parents or your guidance counselor about your list. Maybe they can offer some suggestions.

_____

_____

_____

_____

- Also write down five obstacles standing in the way of getting a sound night's sleep and try to find solutions for them.

_____

_____

_____

_____

9 stop one of the biggest triggers of overeating

Chloe: *Not only am I picky eater, but I also struggle with mindless eating. It's like I can't just eat. I don't know how to do that. I have to be watching television, texting, or surfing the net in order to eat comfortably. Otherwise, I feel anxious.*

for you to know

When you eat while doing other things, it can be very easy to overeat. After all, you're not concentrating on your food; your mind is elsewhere. Not only does this mean you won't realize how much you're eating, but you also won't really be able to enjoy the experience.

for you to do

The next time you have a snack, try this activity: a mindful meal.

1. Remind yourself that it is okay to have a snack when you are genuinely hungry.

2. Before you eat, rate your hunger level from 1 to 10, with 1 being ravenous and 10 being stuffed. Where are you?

3. Create a distraction box. Get a box the size of a shoe box. Before your meal, ask your dining companions to be part of a mindful meal. Pass the box around, and have everyone put his or her phone inside. If you're alone, just put in yours. Set the box aside. Not being able to see the phone will help take away the urge to automatically reach for it.

4. Turn off as many distractions as you can. Sit at a table. Turn off the television. If you can't remove some distractions (such as a television that is on in a restaurant), just be mindful of their place.

5. Pay attention to how it feels to eat without distraction. Uncomfortable? Boring? Relaxing? Focused?

You don't have to eat in silence everytime you eat, but hopefully this exercise will make you do a three-second check anytime you eat to be aware of how distractions may be impacting you.

more to do

When you eat, just eat! Let this be your motto for one week. Let's make a plan for this week for reducing your distraction. Here is an example:

Day 1: No eating while driving or in the car.

Day 2: No eating while watching television.

Day 3: No eating while texting or on the phone.

Day 4: No eating while doing homework or while working.

Day 5: No eating while walking or standing.

Day 6: No eating while using a computer or other electronic devices or games.

Day 7: Choose your own: no eating while _____…

Now, write out your own plan for seven days.

Day 1: _____

Day 2: _____

Day 3: _____

Day 4: _____

Day 5: _____

Day 6: _____

Day 7: _____

journal exercise

Once you've tried this for a week, write about your experience.

- Which day was the most challenging to eat without distraction?

_____

_____

- Which was the easiest?

_____

_____

- Eating without distractions makes me feel…

_____

_____

- I am the most distracted when I eat (for example, with friends, with family, on the bus, in the subway)…

_____

_____

- I notice the urge to eat when I am (for example, studying, watching television)…

_____

_____

10 what to be mindful of in nutrition labels

Thalia: *I don't think I realized that food came with an ingredients list until I had to buy some gluten-free food for a friend. It was such an eye-opening experience! Not only did it seem that everything contained gluten, but there were also all these ingredients I'd never heard of and couldn't even pronounce. When I started doing some research on them, I realized that a lot of what I was eating wasn't good for my health at all. It was a lot of chemicals.*

for you to know

There's a difference between whole food and junk food, but it's sometimes not easy to tell the difference—and packaging doesn't make it any easier. When your parents or caregivers bring food into the house—onions, carrots, packaged snack cakes, and soda—it's all the same thing, right? It's edible, so it's food. Not necessarily. Let's take a closer look. Taking even a quick glance at a nutrition label can be eye-opening!

for you to do

Start reading food labels. Encourage your family to do the same. When you read food labels, you'll gain a better understanding of why some foods make you feel full and alert and why others make you feel groggy and nauseated after you eat them. The goal is not to obsess over the calories, but to understand what you are putting in your body and how it makes you feel.

To get you started on this process, go get one of your favorite food items right now (preferably one that comes with nutritional information). If it doesn't have it, you can look up the information online. Turn it over and scan the nutrition label for a minute.

- Look at the portion size. What do you notice? Is the portion size in line with how much of this food you would normally eat? For example, let's say a serving of potato chips is one-quarter of a cup of chips. Rarely does anyone eat just a few chips.

- Look at the ingredients list. Is it long or short? Which ingredients are you happy to see? Which ingredients concern you?

- How much nutritional value does this provide to you? A lot? Not much? Look at the percentages to understand.

- What symbols or other information do you notice? Is it free of genetically modified ingredients, organic, or vegetarian? Does it contain artificial sweeteners?

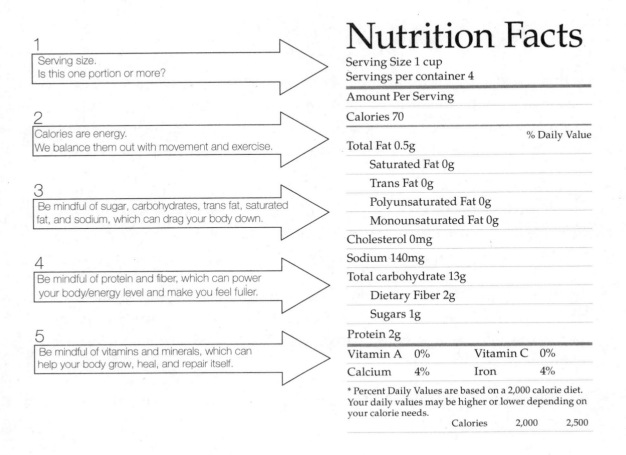

1
Serving size.
Is this one portion or more?

2
Calories are energy.
We balance them out with movement and exercise.

3
Be mindful of sugar, carbohydrates, trans fat, saturated fat, and sodium, which can drag your body down.

4
Be mindful of protein and fiber, which can power your body/energy level and make you feel fuller.

5
Be mindful of vitamins and minerals, which can help your body grow, heal, and repair itself.

Nutrition Facts

Serving Size 1 cup
Servings per container 4

Amount Per Serving

Calories 70

% Daily Value

Total Fat 0.5g

    Saturated Fat 0g

    Trans Fat 0g

    Polyunsaturated Fat 0g

    Monounsaturated Fat 0g

Cholesterol 0mg

Sodium 140mg

Total carbohydrate 13g

    Dietary Fiber 2g

    Sugars 1g

Protein 2g

Vitamin A	0%	Vitamin C	0%
Calcium	4%	Iron	4%

* Percent Daily Values are based on a 2,000 calorie diet. Your daily values may be higher or lower depending on your calorie needs.

	Calories	2,000	2,500

Figure 3. **A Nutrition Label**

Now that you have become more mindful of food labels, pick one nutrient that is important to you. If you're active in sports, you may choose protein, for example (teenage boys need about fifty-two grams a day and teenage girls about forty-six grams). Make it a goal for a week to record how much protein is in the foods you are eating. Or if you have a sweet tooth, you might choose to be mindful of added sugar in foods. You will be surprised how much sugar is hidden in everyday foods like ketchup!

In the chart below, specify what nutrient or additive you are tracking and note how much of it is in your meals for a week. For example, Thalia recorded how much protein was in the yogurt she had for breakfast, her chicken sandwich at lunch, and so forth.

Nutrient: _____

	Mon	Tues	Wed	Thurs	Fri	Sat	Sun
Breakfast							
Lunch							
Snacks							
Dinner							

more to do

It's not just what is in your food that's important; where it comes from is also key. The next time you pick up a banana at the store or at home, check out the sticker on it. It's likely from thousands of miles away: Chile, Mexico, Argentina. It took a lot for that banana to get from where it was grown to you. Why is that important? Knowing where food comes from not only makes you appreciate it more but it also helps you to understand what is in it and how it was grown.

journal exercise

It's time to journal about your experiences.

- When I looked at the nutrition labels, I felt...

_____

_____

- When I kept track of the nutrient or additive _____ in my food, I was surprised that...

_____

_____

- In the future, what I will look for on labels is...

_____

_____

Marco: *Whenever I have food in front of me, I feel like I have to eat it all. I usually feel guilty afterward, because I'm already overweight. I don't know how all the guys around me turn what they eat into muscle. All I seem to do is get a rounder middle. I know I need to control my eating, but I just can't get a grip on it.*

for you to know

Nearly everyone has done it at least once: You want to eat a few potato chips, so you grab the package, and the next thing you know, you've eaten the entire bag. Instead of eating a little something to take the edge off your hunger until the next meal, you've filled up on snack food and have no room left over for a nourishing meal.

for you to do

To make sure a snack stays a snack, you can use what you already know about mindful eating. The key points are easy to remember: just think of *SNACK*.

S—Slow down! Consciously choose a snack. Sometimes we just eat what's there and handy rather than actively and intentionally choosing something that is tasty and reduces hunger.

N—Notice your hunger level (on the scale from 1 to 10).

A—Ask yourself, *What are my options?*

C—Choose thoughtfully. Ask yourself, *Will this meet my needs—will it take the edge off my hunger or craving?*

K—Kindness. As you eat your snack, ask yourself, *Am I being kind to my body right now? Should I stop right now or keep eating?* If you want more, pick up another chip and ask the same thing. Continue with each chip until the bowl is empty—or until your answer is *Stop*.

more to do

Remember that it's fine and healthy to have a snack! It's helpful to have them portioned out and ready to go. This week, your challenge is to create a mindful snack grab bag specifically for the time you are most likely to snack. We like things that are convenient and ready to go. For example, if you tend to have a snack after school, portion out a snack the night before or in the morning, put it in a bag with your name on it, and stick it in the refrigerator or on the counter. So when you get home, your snack is waiting for you. This also helps to reduce grabbing whatever is near and gives you time to mindfully create a satisfying option. Or create a snack grab bag for your backpack that you can take with you for after school or before practice.

There are a wide variety of snacks that give you energy and satisfy hunger:

- hard-boiled eggs

- string cheese

- almonds or trail mix

- hummus and pretzels

- peanut butter and apples

- yogurt and homemade smoothies

- berries, apples, bananas, oranges, or grapes

- popcorn sprinkled with Parmesan cheese

- corn chips and bean dip or avocado slices

- granola

- graham crackers with vanilla yogurt

- dark chocolate (if seeking something sweet) or sprinkle on some chocolate chips

- cheese cubes and jerky

It's helpful to brainstorm about what you would like to include. You may need to talk to an adult about making sure these foods are on hand and the best time to eat them. Answer this prompt—my mindful snack grab bag would include these three things:

_____

_____

_____

journal exercise

Journal about your experience.

- The snack that makes me feel the most satisfied is... _____

_____

_____

- The food I tend to reach for as a snack is... _____

_____

_____

- I crave... _____

_____

_____

- Tonight, I put my snack into a small bowl and ate only that snack. This made me feel...

_____

_____

- Tomorrow, I'm going to...

_____

_____

Mood

One important aspect of mindful eating is mood. Mindless eating is often the result of a mood you're in but are not completely aware of. Imagine that you're stressed about finishing a school project. Instead of feeling anxious, you automatically crave something sweet, like a cupcake, or something comforting, like a bowl of mashed potatoes. There is no conscious thought involved: *I'm stressed, so I want to eat a cupcake*. It's just an immediate craving that follows the mood.

In this section of the workbook , you'll learn how to better connect with your emotions so you understand them more fully and so they don't control your habits. You'll also learn why stress and food are so closely linked and what you can do to soothe yourself without food.

12 identify emotional eating versus physical hunger

Emma: *Sometimes I think I'm hungry, but actually I'm just super bored. I'm not really hungry, but I'll wander into the kitchen and snack on something for a while. I did this yesterday. I know I wasn't really hungry, because nothing sounded good to me.*

for you to know

There are two types of hunger: physical and emotional. But the tricky thing is that your emotions—sadness, fear, anger—can actually feel like physical hunger. Sometimes the ache you feel doesn't mean that your body needs fuel; it's your mind telling you it needs comfort—rest, relaxation, or a hug from a friend. Once you learn the difference between these two kinds of hunger, you'll be able to tell if your body is asking for nourishment or your emotions are asking for comfort. Let's take a look at both types in detail.

Physical Hunger	Emotional Hunger
When your body needs nourishment, you will feel an emptiness in your stomach. You may feel your tummy rumbling. Other symptoms of physical hunger are fatigue, shakiness, and sometimes irritability.	When your emotions need comfort, you will feel a pang in your heart or a knot in your stomach. You may feel the urge to cry or rage. Other symptoms of emotional hunger include cravings for sweet foods, the urge to binge eat, and the desire to "stuff" your feelings rather than face them.

Here is a chart to help you recognize the signs of physical and emotional hunger.

PHYSICAL vs. EMOTIONAL
H U N G E R

PHYSICAL
- Stomach growling/low energy
- Thinking/considering options
- Low energy
- Hunger grow slowly
- Time has passed since last meal
- Food is satisfying

EMOTIONAL
- No physical cues (quiet stomach)
- Specific cravings (like chocolate)
- Eating food feels like the best/only option
- Little time has passed since last bite
- Food doesn't totally satisfy
- Wandering around kitchen/searching for food

YES

EAT

Healthy   **Unhealthy**

Eat it mindfully

NO

Distraction   **Comfort**

Distraction	Comfort
Get out of kitchen	Relax
Keep hands busy	Breathe deeply
Connect	Sleep/lie down
Clean	Unplug from electronics
Read	Connect/be social
Exercise/move	Soothe body
Mindless activity	Wear comfy clothing

for you to do

The practice of mindful eating is a great way to learn to tell the difference between physical and emotional hunger. The next time you feel an urge to eat, really listen to what your body is telling you. Ask yourself these five mindful questions. Make a fist with one hand. Assign each question to one finger. As you answer each one, hold up that finger.

- Thumb—When was the last time I ate?
  - ✳ Physical: Several hours ago (a general guideline is three hours after a full meal).
  - ✳ Emotional: I just ate.

- Index—Where is the hunger coming from? What triggered this desire for food?
  - ✳ Physical: My stomach rumbled.
  - ✳ Emotional: I am feeling stressed and just wandered into the kitchen.

- Middle—What would satisfy me?
  - ✳ Physical: Any kind of a snack would satisfy me.
  - ✳ Emotional: I am having a craving for something specific, and only that food item will do.

- Ring—What am I feeling right now?
  - ✳ Physical: Low energy, stomach rumbling.
  - ✳ Emotional: Sad, anxious, or bored.

- Pinky—What are my options?
  - ✳ Physical: Do I want a meal or just a snack?
  - ✳ Emotional: Do I want to talk with someone or go for a run to relieve my stress?

Now your hand should be open and ready to pick an option. Asking yourself these questions doesn't mean you have to change anything about the way you respond to these feelings right now. Just be aware of them and work with them. Becoming familiar with how hungry you are will give you an idea of whether you need fuel or a way to calm and soothe your nerves.

more to do

5–5–5–5–5 Activity

Avoid emotional eating by having a solid plan in place. Write down a list of five strategies for each category. Hang these sheets in hot spots for emotional eating, like on your desk or refrigerator.

Five *activities* that relax you (flipping through a magazine, a five-minute break, lying on the couch).

1. _____

2. _____

3. _____

4. _____

5. _____

Five *activities* that distract you (email, games, cleaning).

1. _____

2. _____

3. _____

4. _____

5. _____

Five *places* you can go that are comforting to you (your bed, the garden, or a cozy chair).

1. _____

2. _____

3. _____

4. _____

5. _____

Five *people* to connect with (your best friend, mother, sister, or mentor).

1. _____

2. _____

3. _____

4. _____

5. _____

Five *things* that soothe your senses (a cool cloth on your forehead, comfortable clothing, or turning down the lights).

1. _____

2. _____

3. _____

4. _____

5. _____

journal exercise

Journaling will help you get a good handle on how your body lets you know when you are emotionally versus physically hungry.

- I become the most physically hungry when I [am playing sports, get up in the morning]…

_____

_____

- My body lets me know that I am physically hungry by these cues [I have low energy, my stomach rumbles, I have a headache]…

_____

_____

- The foods that help to reduce my physical hunger best are [list some foods that help you feel full longer, like nuts, fruit, or granola bars]…

_____

_____

- The feelings that trigger the most emotional eating are [boredom, stress]…

_____

_____

- The situations that trigger the most emotional eating are [exams, arguments with friends]…

_____

_____

13 cope with your cravings

Jayden: *There are a few foods I crave all the time. I love chocolate—anything chocolate. I could eat it any time of the day or night. I know I eat too much of it.*

for you to know

Even if you're not physically hungry, you crave certain foods. This is normal, and it happens to all of us. If you see a picture of a chocolate cake or watch a show in which one of the characters is eating popcorn, you might find yourself craving these foods. When you experience this kind of craving, it is good to ask yourself if you're physically hungry or if simply being reminded of a particular food made you want it.

for you to do

There are several easy steps that can help you cope with cravings.

Step one: Ask yourself why you really want it. Are you hungry? Do you just want the taste? Are you bored? Feeling deprived of a certain food? Just asking yourself why you crave a particular food can help you determine the way to respond to that craving.

Step two: If there is something you are particularly craving, mindfully answer that craving by getting a portion of it (if you crave chocolate, enjoy a reasonable portion of it).

Step three: Practice! Practice eating the foods you love and crave in a mindful way, so you don't go overboard with them. Anything that you do intentionally and repeatedly, you learn to do well. Think about the types of practice you do each day, like piano or soccer. You only get better with practice—mindful eating is no different.

The next time you have a craving for something sweet, satisfy that craving and practice the skills you've learned in this book by mindfully eating a small piece of candy:

- Unwrap the candy slowly.

- Notice its texture and color.

- Smell it, and put it in your mouth.

- Chew it carefully, and swallow.

Now check in with yourself. How do you feel?

_____

_____

_____

_____

more to do

Try the four D's of coping with cravings.

Determine: Figure out what your triggers are, and write them below.

- _____
- _____
- _____

Delay: When you experience a craving, check the time. Wait just five minutes. See if the craving passes.

Distract: In that five minutes, distract yourself with an activity. List three ways to distract yourself.

- _____
- _____
- _____

Decide: Decide what you really want. If you want the food you crave, go for it. If you aren't sure, choose a healthier alternative.

Craving	Healthier Alternatives
Chips	Popcorn, veggie chips
Chocolate	Dark chocolate, hot cocoa, chocolate milk
Ice cream	Frozen yogurt, Greek yogurt
Pizza	Make your own pizza, turkey pepperoni
Candy	Frozen fruit (put grapes in freezer)
Milkshake	Smoothies

Journal about your cravings to get to know them. Write down the three foods you crave the most. Then, after each one, brainstorm about how you can make answering that craving just a little more mindful. For example, if you crave chocolate, you might get some one-ounce squares of high-quality chocolate. Give yourself permission to have a square a day, eaten mindfully. Remember that whenever you deprive yourself of something, you simply want it more. Learning how to give yourself what you want in a healthy way is key.

- _____

_____

_____

_____

- _____

_____

_____

_____

- _____

_____

_____

_____

journal exercise

Describe your experience of mindfully answering a craving.

- Describe your experience in detail. How did the craving start? Where did it come from (seeing or smelling a particular food, daydreaming about it)?

_____

_____

- When I have a craving, I feel… _____

_____

- Today, I saw _____, and I satisfied my craving for it by… _____

_____

- Mindfully answering my cravings made me feel… _____

_____

- Tomorrow, I'm going to pay more attention to… _____

_____

stress relief to prevent comfort eating

Thalia: *I'm a naturally anxious person, so I'm pretty much stressed all the time unless I'm sleeping. Ever since I've expanded the kind of foods I eat, I've noticed that cookies, cake, and ice cream give me this relieved kind of feeling after I eat them. Eating = Zen, relaxed feeling.*

for you to know

It's understandable that you reach for food when you are stressed. Food does bring on good feelings. Unfortunately, when you eat to comfort your emotions and cope with stress, you're putting your attention in the wrong place. If you feel anxious because you think you will do poorly on tomorrow's math quiz, eating may temporarily calm you down, but it won't fix the problem. Sometimes we respond to emotion in helpful ways, and sometimes our actions make it worse. There are better ways to cope with stress that last longer. Consider these examples:

- Judy is sad because her best friend, Sarah, is moving away.

  * *Positive response:* She takes a long walk to clear her head and think about all the good times she and Sarah had together. This helps boost her mood.

  * *Negative response:* She eats three cupcakes and gets so sick that she can't get out of bed to see Sarah off the next day. This turns her sadness into guilt.

- Billy shoved Glenn and sent him crashing into a locker after last period.

  * *Positive response:* Glenn stayed after school and swam laps in the pool to calm his anger. He now feels more in control of his emotions.

  * *Negative response:* Glenn tackled Billy and beat him up in the hallway. Now they're both suspended. Glenn feels foolish for letting Billy get to him like that.

for you to do

Now is an important time in your life to learn how to relieve stress without eating. Below are ten ways to relieve stress without taking a single bite. Review this list and put a check mark next to the strategies that may work for you.

☐ *Face your feelings.*

One of the most empowering things you'll ever learn to do in life is face your feelings and not run away from them. If you're sad, allow yourself to feel sad. If you're angry, let yourself be angry. There's nothing wrong with any emotion you feel. What's important is your *response* to emotion—which can either solve your problem or cause more problems.

☐ *Mindfully distract yourself.*

The only difference between mindless distraction and mindful distraction is intention. Mindless distraction is watching Netflix for hours on end and shoveling handfuls of snacks into your mouth while completely ignoring your emotions.

Mindful distraction is watching a movie on Netflix without doing anything else (eating, texting, and so forth) to give yourself a break for a while. It's being completely caught up in the plot of the movie and enjoying some carefree time.

The next time you feel emotional hunger, try a mindful distraction. Watch a movie, read a few chapters of a book, or play a computer game for half an hour. Whatever you choose to do, focus on it to the exclusion of all else until the time you've allotted yourself is up.

☐ *Call a friend.*

Sometimes it's hard to process what you're feeling all by yourself. Talking to a friend or close relative can help you get some perspective.

☐ *Work on a project.*

Another way to distract yourself from a pesky craving is to work on a project. This is doubly beneficial if you do something you've been putting off for a while. Not only will the food craving vanish, but you'll also walk away with a sense of accomplishment.

☐ *Exercise.*

If you're feeling anxious or angry, going for a hike, a jog, or a swim can be a great way to release those emotions. When you're done, not only will you be carrying a lighter emotional load, but you'll also feel more healthy and confident. Now that's a win-win!

☐ *Play with your pet.*

Pets are wonderful distractions, and studies have shown they can really help relieve stress. Don't have a pet? Ask your neighbors if you can borrow theirs for a bit, or volunteer at your local shelter.

☐ *Take a soothing bath.*

A warm, relaxing bath can help ease the tension in your muscles and release stress. While you're at it, take a good book in there with you, and let your anxiety ebb away.

☐ *Change your surroundings.*

We humans were not designed to sit as much as we do, so it's easy to get antsy when you've been in one place too long. If you're feeling a strong emotional craving, but you're not physically hungry, see if changing your surroundings helps. Getting back into nature is always a good way to calm your senses and reconnect with yourself.

☐ *Have a good cry.*

When you feel sad, anxious, or even angry, sometimes the best thing you can do is go to a quiet place where you won't be disturbed and have a good cry. Studies have shown that the tears shed from an emotional trigger (rather than from something like allergies) contain stress chemicals that are leaving the body.

☐ *Write about how you feel.*

When you feel overwhelmed with emotion, it can be difficult to pin down exactly what is causing your heart to pound, your stomach to knot up, or your muscles to tense. Writing about your day can help you find the root cause of your feelings. Pinpointing the problem can give you some perspective, which can help you find a way to solve the problem—or at least it can relieve the emotions you're feeling.

☐ *Other:* _____

_____

_____

_____

more to do

Look at the strategies listed above. Create a bingo-style board of activities that you find comforting and soothing. Fill in the blank spots. Copy this and hang it up in an easy to see location. Commit to doing one of these activities every day this week. Hey, we need soothing every day, don't we? Put a sticker on the activity after you have tried it.

R	E	L	A	X
		Exercise, move, stretch		
				Sip herbal tea
Call a friend		Listen to music		
	Take a hot bath			

journal exercise

Describe the experience.

- The activity that helped me the most to stay calm and relieve stress was…

_____

_____

_____

_____

_____

- The challenges I faced when attempting these new strategies were…

_____

_____

_____

_____

_____

ways to boost your energy (without caffeine)   15

Jayden: *Classes are tough. I used to drink energy drinks all the time to keep up with my classes and part-time job. They made me shaky, and I felt terrible. I tried switching back to coffee, but it just made me so nervous that I would feel sick. Recently, I've learned how to boost my energy levels without any food or drink, and it's starting to work really well for me.*

for you to know

Jayden has the right idea. You don't need any type of food or drink to boost your energy levels. Once you make the connection between certain physical activities and a boost in energy, you'll realize you don't need to take anything *into* your body; you just have to *use* your body. This is one of the best ways to boost your mood and feel more energized.

for you to do

The next time you feel your energy lagging, try the following exercises:

Stretch Your Chest.

Stand in a doorway and place your palms flat against the wall on either side of the door frame. Keep your back straight. Lean forward through the doorway without moving your hands. You should feel a stretch across your chest. Move your hands higher or lower to stretch different areas of your chest.

Stretch Your Arms.

Stand facing a wall. Place your right hand flat against the wall for balance, and lift your left leg slightly so that your weight is on your right leg. Tighten your abdominal muscles, and keep your back straight. Lightly touch the fingers of your left hand to your right armpit, then reach out and up until your left arm is reaching straight overhead, fingers pointing toward the ceiling. Keep your right shoulder blade down. Hold for five seconds and repeat ten to fifteen times. Switch sides.

Breathe Faster.

This will get your oxygen pumping. When you have some time to yourself, sit down, and breathe in and out rapidly through your nose for a minute or two. If you have anxiety or feel dizzy, slow your breathing and take a series of deep breaths instead.

Change Your Scenery.

Your senses get used to your room, your school, and the mall. Wake them up by changing your surroundings. Go for a walk outside, take a swim, or just sit back and watch the clouds roll by.

Wake Up Your Legs.

While you're watching the clouds roll by, lie down. Raise one leg and then the other until they are both in the air. Now, shake them for a minute or two. (If you feel strange doing it by yourself, invite your little brother or sister to do it with you. They'll love it!)

Stand Up More.

Sitting too long can drain your energy and even make you feel sick. So take every opportunity you can to stand up and get that blood flowing!

Give Yourself a Massage.

Using your hands, gently knead out the tension in your shoulders. You can also massage your feet by rolling them over a frozen water bottle or a tennis ball. Self-massage is relaxing and energizing.

more to do

There are many more ways to increase your energy and reduce the things that are sucking you dry. Our energy is tapped in a lot of different ways. Take a quick assessment of the ways that the strategies in the first column alter your energy level. Each day, commit to reducing one of the energy drainers or engage in a booster. Below is an example, followed by a blank chart for you to use.

	Energy Boosters	Energy Drainers
Physical (sleep, nutrition, exercise, hydration)	I could sleep an extra hour, take vitamins	Sugary snacks zap my energy in the afternoon
Emotional (stress, conflict, kindness, friendship)	Time with Jason	Less time with Jessica
Mental (packed schedule, multitasking, boredom, stress, homework, taking breaks, distraction)	Volunteering	Procrastinating on homework leaves me stressed
Spiritual (prayer, gratitude, being positive, kind acts, engaging in meaningful things)	Say a prayer each night, make a list of things I am grateful for	Feeling guilty

	Energy Boosters	Energy Drainers
Physical (sleep, nutrition, exercise, hydration)		
Emotional (stress, conflict, kindness, friendship)		
Mental (packed schedule, multitasking, boredom, stress, homework, taking breaks, distraction)		
Spiritual (prayer, gratitude, being positive, kind acts, engaging in meaningful things)		

journal exercise

Write about how the activities you tried made you feel. You can use the prompts below to help you get started

- The activity that boosts my energy the most is…

- The people and places that drag down my energy level are…

- When my energy level is down, I tend to naturally want to _____, but a better option is to _____.

- Tomorrow, I'll try…

_____

_____

_____

_____

_____

_____

boost your mood with food   16

Thalia: *Stress has always been my number one reason to overeat. I know it's important to realize that eating can't solve my problems, and, sometimes, it only makes things worse. But I did learn that there are certain foods that can boost my mood naturally, and I'm definitely ready to try that!*

for you to know

If you are feeling blue or stressed and want to turn that feeling around, there are some foods to consider adding to your diet. Studies show that foods packed with vitamins and minerals help you to fight fatigue, brighten your mood, and get you through those frustrating hours of sitting in front of your computer doing homework. So the next time you feel that irritating, pesky slump in your mood, try reaching for a natural energy booster. It's one of the best ways to brighten your mood.

for you to do

Let's take a look at some of the more common nutrient deficiencies and the benefits each nutrient can offer to boost your mood naturally. First, let's see how much you know already. Grab a pencil and try to match the nutrient with its benefits by drawing a line from one to the other in the chart below. (Don't worry. The answers are on the next page.)

| Magnesium | 1. | There are eight of these vitamins. This one plays an important role in converting food into fuel, allowing you to stay energized. It's essential for healthy skin, hair, and nails. |

Vitamin D   2.   A deficiency in this mineral can cause anemia, which may lead to fatigue, apathy, and depression.

Iron   3.   This essential fatty acid helps brain development, reduces inflammation, and helps your heart by lowering blood pressure.

Calcium   4.   This vitamin helps the body to produce and maintain new cells. It also helps prevent birth defects.

Folic acid   5.   This vitamin helps to calm your nervous system and keep it healthy. It also aids digestion and keeps your brain cells communicating with each other well.

Omega-3   6.   This mineral is critical to increasing energy, calming nerves and muscles, sleeping well, and maintaining your energy level.

Zinc   7.   This "sunshine vitamin" helps you beat the winter blues.

Chromium   8.   This mineral helps improve digestion and balance hormones and aids growth. Deficiencies lead to poor concentration and reduces your ability to heal wounds.

Vitamin B_6 9.   This mineral helps build strong bones. Furthermore, a lack of it may lead to PMS-related depression.

Vitamin B_{12} 10.   This mineral helps to regulate your blood sugar and helps you metabolize and digest food.

Answer Key:

1. Vitamin B_{12}. Sources include milk, beef, chicken, Swiss cheese, and eggs.

2. Iron. Sources include beef, turkey, and lentils.

3. Omega-3. Sources include salmon and some other kinds of fish, chia seeds, and spinach.

4. Folic acid. Sources include spinach, black-eyed peas, and avocado.

5. Vitamin B_6. Sources include fish, nuts, beef, turkey, beans, and eggs.

6. Magnesium. Sources include dark chocolate, avocados, nuts, chickpeas, and peas.

7. Vitamin D. Sources include eggs, salmon, and milk.

8. Zinc. Sources include roasted pumpkin seeds, cashews, and Swiss cheese.

9. Calcium. Sources include collard greens, yogurt, and ricotta cheese.

10. Chromium. Sources include broccoli, organic grape juice, and mashed potatoes.

How many did you get right?

more to do

Now let's try to diversify your diet and increase your nutrition level. It's one of the best ways to recharge your mood. One way to do so is to increase the variety of colors in the foods you eat. Many people get stuck in a colorless rut of pale foods—French fries, bread, and so forth. Adding color to your meals increases your access to different nutrients. Consider having a Reset Your Mood Rainbow Day. For each meal, choose at least *three* colors from the rainbow. For example, for breakfast you might have eggs (yellow) and strawberries and blueberries (red and blue). In the chart below, track your meals and take note of your mood.

Rainbow Reset!			
	Breakfast	Lunch	Dinner	Snack
Red				
Orange				
Yellow				
Green				
Blue				
Purple				
How do I feel?				

journal exercise

Now it's time to journal and explore how this activity has helped.

- Today, I tried the following mood-boosting foods… _____

_____

- My favorite color of food is… _____

_____

- The food that makes me feel the best is… _____

_____

- I ate my mood-boosting foods mindfully by… _____

_____

- Tomorrow, I will try… _____

_____

_____

17 creating a self-talk shield

Theresa: *I'm really hard on myself. My friends tell me that I get down on myself too much. I say mean stuff to myself and call myself awful names.*

for you to know

Sometimes we are hard on ourselves. It comes from this little judge-and-jury in the back of your mind that likes to pop up and give its opinion on everything you do—including your food choices. That inner critic is not helpful—it likes to criticize, point out what you did wrong, and tell you what you "should" have done. Unfortunately, it doesn't help you to make better choices. It just leaves you feeling ashamed and guilty. While we can't entirely eliminate the inner critic, we can stop giving ourselves permission to put ourselves down.

for you to do

Here is where being mindful can step in. Once you start to be more observant and aware of your inner critic, you can start responding to it in a different way. There are several methods that can help.

The Four C's

When your inner critic starts to speak up, remember the four C's.

Catch: Be mindful. Just notice. Say hello to your inner critic: *Hello, inner critic, there you are again!* To lighten it up, you can even give your inner critic a name: *Hello Miss Thinks-She-Know-Everything!*

Curious: Be curious; don't respond with more criticism. Ask yourself where that negative thought came from. Is that your voice speaking, or does it sound like your mother's, a friend's, or a teacher's voice? Ask yourself, *So what?*

Choose: Remember that there is a difference between a thought and a fact. Just because you think it doesn't mean it's true. At this juncture, you have a choice. You can recognize it as just a thought and let it go, or you can believe it or respond to it.

Challenge with Compassion: Talk back! Argue with that inner voice and give some solid reasons why its opinion is too negative. Respond in a way that gives the criticism a more positive spin. If you can't be positive, at least think of something neutral. If your critic said, *You made a stupid food choice,* respond with *I made a choice that could have been better.* Also, instead of thinking, *I was stupid for eating that,* try something like *I felt stupid when I chose that.* This describes how you felt rather than who you are as a person.

The Self-Talk Shield

How you respond to the inner critic is important. Fill this shield with statements to have on hand when you hear your inner critic snipping at you: *A thought is just a thought; it doesn't mean it's a fact,* and *Other people wouldn't agree with that thought,* and *I am good enough the way I am.*

Figure 4. **The Self-Talk Shield**

92

The "I Am" Wheel

Remembering who you are and what you stand for can keep you motivated. Fill out this wheel.

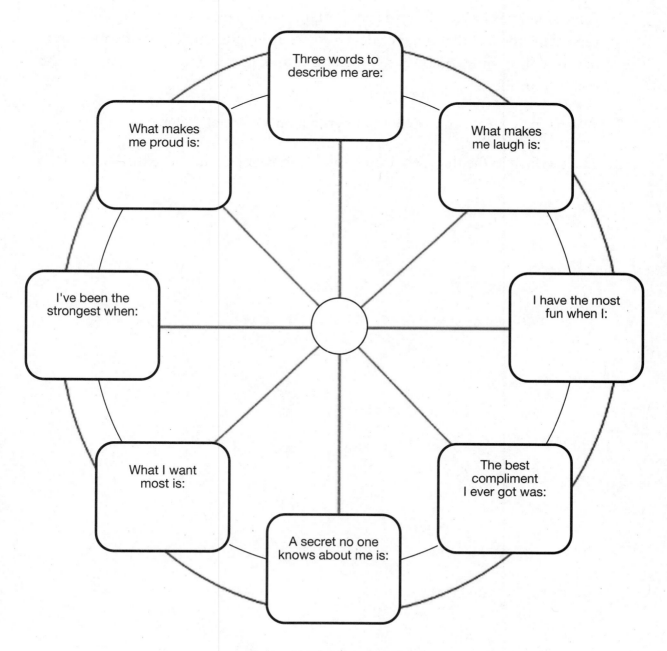

Figure 5. **The I Am Wheel**

more to do

Let's continue to work on letting go of these critical inner thoughts.

1. Get a small box or jar. The size is important. The smallness of the container represents the fact that inner criticism comes from one small part of your mind, not the entire thing. Also, these problems or thoughts are small compared to the rest of your life.

2. When you have a negative thought, write it on a piece of paper.

3. Say goodbye to the thought, drop it into the box or jar, and close the lid. Let it go.

journal exercise

Explore your efforts to deal with your inner critic with this journal exercise.

- What are the three most common things your inner critic says?

_____

_____

_____

_____

_____

- What happens when you respond to each of those statements with compassion or a neutral stance?

_____

_____

_____

_____

_____

18   coping with food pushers

Jayden: *I've been warned to stay away from drug pushers, but I didn't know "food pushers" were even a thing. I mean, that sounds weird, right? I get it, though. And it's hard to say no when somebody offers you something to eat, especially if he made it himself.*

for you to know

For many people, offering food is like offering love. It's also a large part of how we socialize, so eating together is a sign of inclusion. Since most of our gatherings revolve around food, it can be difficult for you to say no to food without feeling awkward or rude, even when you want to. However, it's important that you continue to eat mindfully and tune in to your own body's signals. That means that sometimes you'll want to eat when others aren't, and there may be other times when everyone else is eating, but you're not interested. This doesn't make you strange or weird; it just means that you are getting in touch with your body and what it needs to be nourished. All it takes is some practice on how to say no in a way that is polite but gets your message across loud and clear.

for you to do

In theory, this all sounds great, right? You should make choices based on what your body is telling you. But what do you do when you're at a friend's house for dinner—and you don't want the homemade apple pie, but you don't want to offend your friend's mother? And what do you do when you're out at a pizza place after the football game, and everyone else is eating—but you're not really hungry? As much as you might want to "just say no" to food when you don't really want it, certain situations can be a bit awkward.

Practice Common Scenarios.

The best way to get started is to experiment with possible situations, so you can practice how to gently say no to the food pushers in your life. Read through these scenarios and circle the ones that sound familiar to you.

Scenario 1: *Aunt Maggie and the Apple Pie*

Aunt Maggie: Won't you have a second helping of my homemade apple pie?

You: No, thank you. I'm full. It was delicious, though. Thank you.

Aunt Maggie: You're a growing boy; you need to eat!

You: (*making your hand into a fist*) Did you know this is the actual size of your stomach? It's amazing to think about how much we try to put in there!

Scenario 2: *Uncle Phil and the Inappropriate Comments*

Uncle Phil: You sure can put it away. Girls don't usually eat that much!

You: Ouch! *(In this case, a simple "ouch" might be enough to let your uncle know he's gone a bit too far. But if he keeps going...)*

Uncle Phil: Well, aren't you worried about your figure?

You: Eating like a bird went out of style when all women did was sit around in corsets and hoop skirts. I'm going for a run later!

Scenario 3: *Grandma and the Special Cupcakes*

Grandma: I made these cupcakes especially for you.

You: It was sweet of you to think of me, but I couldn't eat another bite.

Grandma: Well, how about you take some home with you?

You: *(giving Grandma a hug)* Yes, thank you, I'll take them home. That's a perfect solution. I love you and appreciate everything you do for me.

Scenario 4: *The Nosy Neighbor at the Christmas Party*

Nosy Neighbor: Are you sure you should be eating that?

You: *(in a light, matter-of-fact tone, like you're just stating a fact)* Wow. You seem really concerned with what other people are eating. *(There may be an awkward silence at this point, but your message will get through, and you won't have to worry about her asking again!)*

Scenario 5: *Your Best Friend and His Protein*

Best Friend: Man, you're too skinny. You need to eat more beef, chicken, nuts, and cheese and get bulky like me.

You: Nah, I don't mind being on the thin side. I'm not into sports, and I don't need huge muscles to take yearbook photos and play golf.

Best Friend: Yeah, but you want to get a girlfriend, right?

You: If the only thing a girl cares about is big muscles, you can have her. She wouldn't be my type, anyway.

My Ready Responses

Okay, now it is time to practice. These responses need to roll off your tongue easily. Get out your acting skills. Today, your challenge is to say at least three of these responses out loud. You can either stand in front of a mirror and act them out or do it when you're alone in your car or the shower. Your task is to say the responses several times in different tones to hear how they sound—playful, serious, and matter-of-fact.

A Mindful Cartoon

Fill out this cartoon strip for the common scenario you circled. Be sure to include how you will mindfully respond to the food pusher.

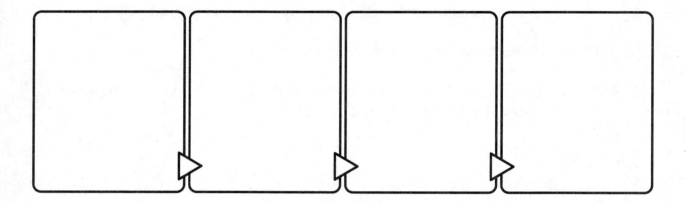

Figure 6. **A Mindful Cartoon**

more to do

In general, it's okay to say no. But saying no to things isn't easy—whether it is food, your best friend, or a fun activity—even when you need to do something else. There are lots of creative ways to say no. Try some of these on for size. How is it easiest for you to say no? Circle the strategy that is likely to work best for you.

Choosing: I choose not to eat that.

Just say no firmly: No, I don't want to eat it.

Rationale: I don't like to eat too many sweets; it gives me a headache.

Not for me: Brownies are just not my thing; I don't like them.

Repeat: I said no already. What part of *no* did you not understand?

Assertive: No, I don't want to eat that, and please take it away.

Polite: No, thank you. But I appreciate the offer.

Value: No thanks. It's not good for my health.

Create your own style of no: _____

Say each of these out loud. Observe how you feel when you say them. Be mindful of your body and your response. Your task is to practice at least three different ways of saying no to something. It doesn't have to be food. The better you get at setting limits in general, the easier it gets to set limits with yourself and others. Then try it in food situations. When you want another helping but aren't really hungry, practice saying no in one of the above manners.

journal exercise

The most important thing for you to remember is that your body, your feelings, and your life are all your own. You are the one in control of what you eat, how your emotions affect you, and how you conduct yourself as a person. Peer pressure is as common as breathing, but once you get comfortable standing your ground, you'll weed out the people who don't have your best interests at heart and be more likely to attract those who do.

Think about some incidents in which you have said no to something and stood your ground, even when it was difficult. Here are some prompts that could get you started.

- Yesterday, _____ offered me _____, and I said…

- The person who is most difficult to say no to is _____, because…

- If I could say what I want to them, it would be _____. The reason I don't is because…

_____

_____

_____

_____

_____

_____

Mindset

Do you believe you can start eating healthier, or do you tell yourself, *It's just too hard*? The answer to this question gives you some insight into your mindset. A mindset is a mental attitude. Someone with a positive, or "growth," mindset has thoughts like *I can do this, I'm on the right track, I can try a different strategy*, and *I am working hard at this*. A negative, or "fixed," mindset can cause setbacks in reaching your goals. Its thoughts are, *It will never work, I'm no good at this*, or *I'm never going to get this*. The good news is that with the right mindset you can train your brain to grow, adapt, and change to meet new challenges, particularly healthy eating. And if right now you feel you have a negative mindset, the even better news is that you can change it. In this section, we'll go step by step and show you how to adopt a mindset that will transform your life!

19 how to build self-confidence

Marco: *I have some extra weight around my middle, and my arms jiggle. I tried working out to add some muscle, but it didn't help, so I just quit. If that isn't bad enough, somebody called me "Jigglypuff" last month—after that Pokémon character—and the name has stuck. My confidence is at an all-time low.*

for you to know

Are you confident? If you answered, "No," or, "Not all the time," that's okay. The good news about confidence is that it is something you can learn. It's a mindset and way of being that you can practice and develop.

Here is what you need to know about confidence: too often, we pin 100 percent of our confidence on our weight—*I'd be happier if I were thinner.* The truth is that you can be confident at any shape and size.

for you to do

On a scale from 1 to 10, with 10 being highest, identify right now how confident you feel. If you need to boost your confidence (if your answer was below 6 or 7), try these twelve activities to start changing your confidence level.

---

12 Days of Self-Confidence

Day 1: Consciously smile at least ten times throughout the day. Body language projects to others how you feel about yourself.

Day 2: Mindfully choose a special outfit that makes you feel comfortable and represents you. Notice how you feel during the day. If you get a compliment, say thank you.

Day 3: Do something new that you have never done before.

Day 4: Give out at least three genuine compliments. We feel good when we make others happy.

Day 5: Write out a list of ten things that make you unique. Hang this list on your mirror.

Day 6: Teach someone something you know how to do well.

Day 7: Be positive! All day, find the positive spin or look for the take-home lesson of each situation.

Day 8: Write a goodbye letter to the things that drag down your self-confidence.

Day 9: Say no to something or someone.

Day 10: Reward yourself with something special.

Day 11: Say yes to opportunity all day (when you can).

Day 12: Spend thirty minutes doing something that you do well.

more to do

Put your hand down on a piece of paper. Draw the outline around it. Above or next to each finger, write down one of these things: what makes you strong, unique, proud, beautiful, and exceptional. When you are feeling low, make a fist and then open your fingers one at a time, thinking through these qualities.

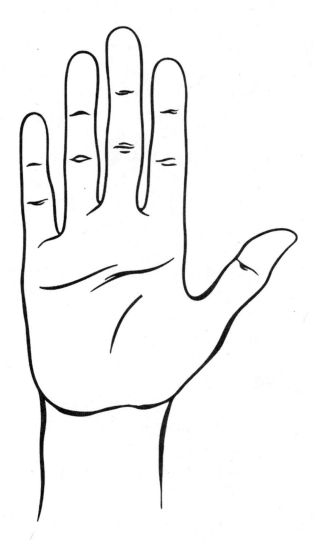

Figure 7. **Your Best Qualities**

journal exercise

Record your thoughts and feelings about the exercises you worked on and how your confidence is growing. Below are some prompts to help get you started.

- As I looked in the mirror today, I noticed my favorite feature is...

- I was able to notice my negative thoughts and change them into positive or neutral ones _____ times today.

- When I do this _____, it makes me feel very self confident, because...

- My self-confidence is worst when I am with _____ and best when I am around _____, because...

_____

_____

_____

_____

_____

_____

20 stop the number one source of unhappiness

Rachel: *Whenever I log on to social media, I get discouraged. There are all these status updates about college scholarships and sports awards and parties, and I'm over here like, "I just ate a whole bag of pretzels in one sitting." Umm... "Go me"?*

for you to know

"Comparison is the thief of joy" is a quote that has most often been attributed to both Christian writer Dwight Edwards and President Theodore Roosevelt. No matter who said it, the statement is true. When you compare yourself with others, it makes you unhappy. It's tempting to compare ourselves in so many different ways—body shape, weight, grades, popularity. The list can go on and on.

for you to do

- *Be Conscious.* Just realizing you are doing it can help you stop it. Sometimes you are comparing yourself to others without even really realizing it. You feel blue and don't even know why. Try grounding yourself. Place your hand on your heart. Feel your heartbeat. Your heartbeat is something that is unique to you. This gesture moves away from your swirling thoughts to focus on what is happening in your body.

- *Don't Give Comparison a Chance.* One of the best things you can do to stop comparing yourself to others is to stop giving yourself so many opportunities to do so. Make it a point to check your social media accounts only every few hours (instead of every few minutes).

- *Challenge the Direction*. With comparison, we are often looking *upward* to people of greater status or *downward* to people of lesser status. When your mind wants to force you to look up or down, instead, look across. Remind yourself, *I am different, not better or worse*. Remember the adage about apples and oranges; they are both fruit but are different from one another. It's totally unfair—even nonsensical—to compare them. Differences make the world unique and interesting. Imagine a world filled with clones who looked exactly the same and had identical abilities— boring! The image could make you laugh a little!

- *Be Realistic*. If you are getting the body image blues from scrolling through social media pages, remind yourself that these images are curated—carefully picked, filtered, or even chosen from a dozen.

- *Limit Your Time*. Because social media can be damaging to your mental and physical health, give yourself a time limit to be on social media. Set a clock.

- *Be a Superhero.* Before you leave the house, stand in a superwoman or superman pose for three minutes—which has been clinically shown to improve your confidence level.

- *Unfollow*. It's perfectly fine to unfollow on social media people who are a detriment to your body image. Simply unfollow or hide them on your feed so their images aren't constantly popping up.

- *Change Your Viewpoint*. If you notice your eyes evaluating how someone looks in their skinny jeans, refocus on something neutral in the room—a piece of artwork or a different person. You control what you see and think about.

- *Compare Yourself to Yourself.* You grow and change each day. Try to be the best version of you.

- *Comfort Is Key.* Squeezing into uncomfortable clothing will make you more conscious of your own body and others in a negative way.

more to do

Save the competition for your sporting events. Instead of competing with others, appreciate and compliment others. When your mind wants to start comparing you to someone, follow these steps. They'll get you to appreciate more and compete less.

1. Simply stop it and say to yourself, *I appreciate* _____ *about her.*

   And follow it up with, *What I appreciate about myself is* _____.

2. Remind yourself, *You are both different, not better or worse.*

3. Refocus your attention in a new direction.

journal exercise

Write about how you compare yourself to others throughout the day and how that makes you feel. Also, try an experiment. Compare yourself…to yourself!

- Four years ago, I had braces on my teeth. Now that they're gone, I feel…

- I was so shy in fifth grade, but nobody would know that now, because…

- I had trouble reading when I was a little kid, and now I'm…

_____

_____

_____

_____

Once you see how far you've already come, it will be that much easier to continue moving in a positive direction.

Use these prompts to continue your journaling exercise.

- One way I could be a little more mindful than I already am is by…

- One activity I already do well is…

- One thing I would like to focus on working hard at is…

_____

_____

_____

_____

21 what to do when you feel fat

Emma: *There are some days when I feel so fat that I don't even want to leave my room. I'm scared other people will make fun of me and know I've gained a couple pounds. It's especially bad when my favorite pair of jeans doesn't fit.*

for you to know

Have you ever said to yourself, *I feel fat*? It's a feeling that we all struggle with at one time or another. Sometimes it's feeling bad about the physical shape of your body. But more often than not, it's really a shorthand way of saying, "I feel bad about myself."

for you to do

Try on a healthier mindset.

- Put the scale away! For one week, vow to stay away from your scale. Hide it. Put it away. Smash it. Whatever you want to do with it. Being tied to the scale can damage your mood and control how you feel from day to day.

- If you can't get rid of the scale, cover up the last number of the scale with a piece of tape. We fluctuate naturally in weight from day to day, but the shift up or down could make or break your mood. Notice how your mindset shifts when it doesn't see an up or down in the last number.

- Tweak your mirror for a day and replace it with a happy picture. Notice how this helps to reduce your looking critically at yourself in the mirror.

- Post your best—not your worst—picture on your refrigerator. Many people put a "fat" picture on their fridge. We often want to shame ourselves into eating better. Research indicates, however, that we are actually more motivated when we feel good about ourselves.

- Fill your Instagram account with healthy messages and images so that what you see is uplifting and inspiring, instead of messages that drag your down—post things like #effyourbeautystandards, #positivebodyimage, and #healthyisthenewskinny.

- Think strong, not skinny. Keep some light weights (like one-pound weights) in your kitchen. Instead of picking up your spoon. This can keep your hands busy.

- Write "Smile!" on small pieces of paper and post them on doorways in your home, where you'll see them as you're passing through. A smile automatically generates a feel-good chemical response.

- Limit your time on social media. Studies show that social media actually makes people feel worse about themselves, because it encourages you to compare yourself to others. If you struggle with comparing yourself with your friends (see activity 20), then limit your time on social media or unfollow people who tug at your self-esteem.

- Vow to stop the diet chitchat. When your friends say negative things about their body, change the subject. Be a good role model. Notice how often this topic comes up in conversation.

- Try to be more descriptive with your feelings. Instead of saying, "I feel fat," try, "I feel stressed today and feel bad about myself" or "I feel uncomfortable in this outfit."

more to do

The next time you're feeling less than comfortable with your body, try the following exercises to beat the Body Blues:

- *Boost your confidence with music.* There are a lot of empowering songs out there to make you feel strong, beautiful, and confident. For example, "Out of the Woods" and "Stay Beautiful" by Taylor Swift, "Beautiful" by Christina Aguilera, "Invincible" by Kelly Clarkson, and "Fight Song" by Rachel Platten.

  What song makes you feel empowered? _____

- *Distraction.* Sometimes, the best thing you can do when you're feeling fat is to distract yourself. Scrolling through social media may make you feel worse because of all the stereotypical images you'll come across. Try this instead: Visit the website www.freerice.com, where you can play games to test your vocabulary or your knowledge of chemistry—or even to prepare for the SAT—and with every click, you are donating free grains of rice to the World Food Programme to combat hunger!

- *Change your clothes.* Are your jeans digging into your belly? Is your top too tight? Change out of those clothes and get into something more comfortable. Put on your favorite sweater or dress, and make yourself feel beautiful.

- *Take a mindful walk.* Once you've changed into some comfortable clothes, take a mindful walk. This will boost your serotonin levels and give you a bit of exercise to increase your confidence. As you walk, focus on the sights, sounds, and smells around you. Really be in the moment, and take everything in.

- *Get in touch with your emotions.* If you're feeling less than confident about your body right now, dig a little deeper. Sometimes you feel fat when you are actually feeling sad, guilty, angry, or hurt. When you become more aware of the thoughts and emotions that lower your self-esteem, you'll be able to process them more quickly, and you will feel better faster.

journal exercise

When you sit down to journal at the end of the day, think about the activities you tried. Which ones made you feel better? Which would you recommend to a friend?

- Today, I felt fat, and I _____. It made me feel...

_____

_____

_____

- Changing into more comfortable clothes made me feel...

_____

_____

_____

- Tomorrow, I will try...

_____

_____

_____

22 do this one thing before you eat

Stacie: *When I'm really stressed or anxious, I just reach for the nearest food available and dive right in. I don't even taste it half the time. It's like I'm just eating it to calm myself down. Sometimes it works, but I hate looking down and realizing that I've devoured a whole package of cookies without even thinking about it.*

for you to know

When you're feeling stressed, it's tough to make decisions. Your body is in fight-or-flight mode, and the only thing it can focus on is fighting or getting you out of danger. That's how our ancestors were able to avoid being eaten by saber-toothed tigers back when we still lived in caves. There was no room for thought in a situation like that, so instinct just took over.

If you're a stress eater, know that your reaction is hard-wired into your biology. It's not a sign of weakness or a lack of willpower. It's a reflex. Making food decisions (or any kind of decision, for that matter) when you're stressed is a no-no. The good news is that you can use mindfulness to change that reflex. Work on pausing and taking a breath before making a food decision so that you don't impulsively reach for food.

for you to do

One of the best ways to calm down is to take a mindful pause. In that pause moment, change the rhythm of your breathing. Draw the symbol below on a piece of paper (or download it from http://www.eatingmindfully.com). When feeling stressed, run your finger along this line and follow the directions for breathing in and out.

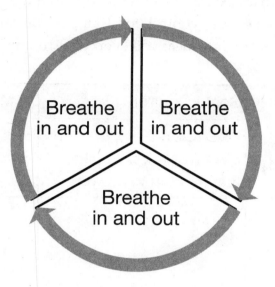

Figure 8. A Mindful Pause

more to do

One of the biggest triggers of stress is trying to change or influence things that are completely out of your control. Evaluate what things you realistically have no control over, what you have some influence over, and what you have 100 percent control over. In your journal (or below), make lists of what in your life fits into these three categories. We've started the table with an example. Continue to fill out the lists with other things in your life that are in or out of your control (for example, you can't control where your family lives, but you can control how neat you keep your room).

Out of My Control	Some Control	In My Control
how many snacks my mom buys at the grocery store	I can ask my mom to buy certain snacks, but she may or may not do it.	the snacks I choose—which snacks and how much I eat

journal exercise

Use the prompts below to explore in more detail how stress impacts your food decisions.

- When I am stressed, I…

- The time of day when I make the best food decisions is… (Note: We tend to make the best food decisions in the morning, before the brain has to make too many decisions for the day.)

- When I feel stressed, the best thing for me to do is…

_____

_____

_____

_____

_____

_____

23 practice mindful movement

Chloe: *I'm a high-energy person, so I need to keep moving, or I feel anxious. I enjoy running, hiking, and swimming, but sometimes I push myself too hard. I train like I'm trying out for the Olympics, and I don't really know why.*

for you to know

I recommend mindful movement rather than "exercise." The word *exercise* makes some people cringe. If you love exercise, that's great! If you don't, start by changing how you look at it. It's likely that you exercise because you "have to"—because it's required in school or because you just feel you must do it. Or perhaps you have set up expectations for yourself that are unrealistic. On the other hand, when you move mindfully, you focus on what feels good—on enjoying the experience—not on burning calories. This is much more healthy than setting up your exercise routine to be unforgiving, inflexible drudgery.

for you to do

For one week, focus on mindful movement.

- If you're hiking, breathe in the fresh air, take in the sights, and feel the trail under your feet—the variety in the terrain, like the unevenness of the rocks and roots and the softness of moss or a meadow.

- If you're swimming, feel yourself gliding through the water, notice the buoyancy of your body, and pay attention to the air rushing in and out of your lungs.

- You can even move mindfully as you go about your day. When you walk up a flight of stairs, feel your feet hitting each step and your thigh muscles working to propel you upward. Or even if you're sitting in a chair—notice how it feels for your feet to be against the floor or your back against the chair.

more to do

Try creating a 5–4–3–2–1 schedule of mindful movement every day. Commit to just fifteen minutes a day of five different activities of your choice—jumping jacks, walking, yoga, or anything else.

5 minutes of _____

4 minutes of _____

3 minutes of _____

2 minutes of _____

1 minute of _____

journal exercise

Record your experiences with mindful movement. Note the differences in the way you feel between competitive exercise and mindful movement.

- My body feels the best when I... _____

_____

- My body feels sore or tired after I have done... _____

_____

- I wish I could do _____, because... _____

_____

- Tomorrow, I plan to... _____

_____

foods that help you focus 24

Marco: *I've always had a rough time concentrating in my classes. My doctor wanted me to try some medication when I was younger, but my parents didn't like that idea. Now we're looking into some natural ways to help me focus.*

for you to know

One of the most important things you need is the ability to focus and concentrate—to do your homework, to play a sport well, or to enhance your performance. One reason you may find focusing a challenge is directly related to the foods you eat, especially junk food, caffeine, and sugar—among some other food culprits. They actually make it difficult for your body to get into a state in which you can relax and pay attention. Even if you're trying to focus, you might find it nearly impossible if the food in your body is fighting you every step of the way.

for you to do

First, let's assess how focused you're feeling right now. Respond to this statement: "Right now I feel…"

☐ Totally focused. Paying close attention.

☐ A bit distracted. Mind wandering from time to time.

☐ Quite distracted. Can't concentrate for very long.

☐ Extremely distracted. Can't concentrate at all; mind is foggy.

If you're overwhelmed or exhausted, you're having difficulty concentrating simply because you're tired. It's time for you to take a break, take a nap, or just go to bed for the night. No amount of caffeine is going to help—and even healthy foods that can help you increase your focus won't do much if your body is downright exhausted.

If you're distracted, but you feel like you still have the energy to keep going, think about what foods you're putting into your body. If you're consuming lots of soda, coffee, energy drinks, or processed or fried foods, you're setting yourself up to fail. Sugary, greasy, and fatty foods might taste good—but later they will make you feel lethargic and slow. Caffeine and sugar do nothing but give you a jolt of energy—only to feel a crash a few hours later. Unfortunately, these foods and drinks will not help you maintain a consistent, steady focus.

more to do

If you struggle with concentration, test how different foods affect you. Keep a record using the image of the two buckets below. For one bucket, write down foods that seem to drain your energy and focus. For the other, write down foods that you notice boost your concentration levels. Before you eat, use the scale in the previous section to establish your concentration level, and then try various foods to see how they affect your energy level.

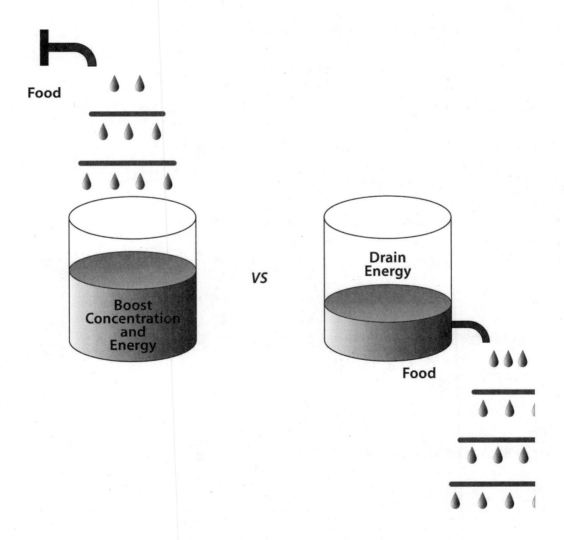

Figure 9. **How Do Different Foods Affect You?**

Performance Foods

If you play sports, compete, or perform in any other events, it's important to power up with snacks. These snacks have been scientifically proven to help you perform better. What drags down your performance (whether it is speed, thinking, strength, or any other ability)? Hunger! Certain foods help with endurance, energy, and mental focus. Try eating one of these options before your next event. Be mindful of how it makes you feel.

- yogurt with fruit and nuts

- peanut butter or almond butter on fruit

- hummus with veggies or whole wheat bread

- low-fat chocolate milk

- homemade trail mix (seeds, raisins, nuts, chocolate)

- fruit, crackers, and cheese

- jerky—a great source of protein and easy to carry

- banana

- grapes

- coconut water

- smoothie with protein powder

- protein bars

The performance-enhancing food I will try is _____.

journal exercise

Write about how trying some of these new foods made you feel. Did your energy level or focus improve? Stay the same? Worsen? It may take a couple of days or a week to notice a big change in your focus, but if you keep eating these and other healthy foods, you'll improve your health in more ways than one. And eating healthier foods can have a ripple effect in your life in other ways—you might feel less guilty about eating junk food, which might make it easier to concentrate.

- When I ate _____, it helped me to...

_____

_____

_____

_____

- The food that ruined my concentration was...

_____

_____

_____

_____

Motivation

In this section of the book, we will take a closer look at motivation. Just like mindset, motivation is an important driving force behind every decision you make, whether it's about food, exercise, or something else. Some days you may wake up full of motivation and vow that today is the day that you are going to make some changes. Then, an hour later, you say to yourself, *Whatever. I don't care.* Motivation can fade as quickly as the sun can disappear behind clouds. In this section, you will read about how to keep your motivation shining bright.

25 mantras and daily motivators

Rachel: *I recently discovered mantras. I felt silly using them at first, but I think they're really starting to help. I'm retraining my brain to stop thinking all the negative thoughts and start being more positive.*

for you to know

Mantras are phrases, quotes, or single words that you repeat to yourself. They stem from an idea that philosophers have known for ages: What you think is what you become. If you have negative thoughts, your outlook and energy level will dim. However, if you shift your mind in a positive direction, you can boost your mood and transform your mindset.

You may have already experienced this boost when you listen to music. Think back to a time that a line from a favorite song got stuck in your head. You kept hearing it all day, didn't you? And because it was a song you loved, it may have lifted your spirits. Similarly, mantras—especially food mantras—are highly effective at putting you in a more positive frame of mind.

- Food is fuel.

- Eat to live; don't live to eat.

- Progress, not perfection.

- I am flexible and flowing.

- I am thankful for this food.

- My body knows what to do with this food. Trust it.

- I love my body as it is today.

- My confidence is growing.

- I know the difference between emotional hunger and physical hunger.

- I am mindful of the food I eat.

for you to do

Copy the list of mantras above, or download it from http://www.eatingmindfully.com, and tape it to your mirror. Read them each day until you have at least five memorized. Even better—make up your own mantras! You can choose a common saying, a verse from a song or poem, a famous quote—anything that gives you a positive mental boost. Then repeat these mantras aloud or in your mind when you feel less than confident or have an emotional food craving—and before and during meals.

more to do

If you are creative, try making a Box of Instant Calm and Motivation.

1. Gather up several small matchboxes or mint boxes that have sliding or removable lids.

2. Cover the outside of one with paper, decorate it, and write on it a thought that often nags at you. For example, *I don't want to do it today.*

3. Then, slide it open and write a motivating quote or mantra on the inside, such as "The best way to get started is to quit talking and begin doing." —Walt Disney.

4. Keep these in places where you often feel you need encouragement: your school locker, your desk, or just your pocket, purse, or backpack. When you need a little boost, just slide one open!

journal exercise

Journal about your experience with mantras.

- My favorite mantra is…

_____

_____

- When I use it, I feel…

_____

_____

- When I first started using mantras, I…

_____

_____

- Tomorrow, I will use the mantra _____
  in the following situations…

_____

_____

26 coping with stuck thinking

Chloe: *Whenever I eat too much, I tell myself that I'm awful. I completely ruined everything, so I might as well keep eating. I wish I could think rationally and say, "Just stop now!"*

for you to know

It's easy to fall into the trap of black-and-white thinking. The situation is all good or all bad, perfect or awful—you get the idea. There is no gray area. What about in your life? Have you witnessed or experienced all-or-nothing thinking? Have you ever heard yourself thinking things like this?

- *I ate perfectly today. I was good today.*

- *I did terribly on my exam. I was completely awful.*

- *I already ate too many chips, so I might as well eat the entire bag.*

for you to do

Look at these examples of black-and-white thinking, and put a check mark next to the ones that are like things you have thought. It's okay if you check a lot of boxes. The idea isn't to be right or wrong (all or nothing!); the idea is to understand the messages your brain might be sending you without you even realizing it.

- ☐ I was making a joke and accidentally upset my friend. She'll never talk to me again.

- ☐ I failed my math quiz. Now I'll never get into the college I wanted to.

- ☐ I ate one cupcake. I might as well eat the rest of them.

- ☐ I forgot to do my chores, and Mom got mad at me. I'm nothing but a screw-up.

- ☐ I came in last in the race today. My running career is over.

- ☐ I backed into the mailbox with my dad's car. He's never going to trust me again.

- ☐ I'm not thin and beautiful like [insert celebrity name]. Nobody will ever ask me out.

- ☐ My belly is too big. I know everyone sees it and wonders if I'm pregnant.

- ☐ I'm a guy who has a crush on another guy. If anybody finds out, they'll hate me.

- ☐ I had a sip of beer for the first time today. I'm going to become an alcoholic.

Think about how the statements above made you feel. Did you have a knot in your stomach? Did your chest feel tight? Black-and-white thinking can feel similar to the fight-or-flight response we experience when we're in danger.

The statements made me feel _____.

Let's take a look at these statements again, but after they've been phrased a bit differently.

I was making a joke and accidentally upset my friend. I should apologize to her.

I failed my math quiz. I'll have to study harder next time.

I ate one cupcake, and it was delicious. I can save the rest for later.

I forgot to do my chores, and Mom got mad at me. I'll set reminders on my phone.

I came in last in the race today. I'll train harder and do better in the next race.

I backed into the mailbox with my dad's car. I'll use my allowance to pay to have the dent fixed.

I'm beautiful just the way I am. If somebody can't see it, he's not the right one.

Everyone's stomach is rounded. It's never perfectly flat.

I'm a guy who has a crush on another guy. I can't be afraid to be who I am.

I had a sip of beer for the first time today. It was okay, but not something I'd do again.

How did you feel about the statements this time? Did you feel calmer and more in control of your emotions?

The statements made me feel _____.

Words like *always, never, perfect, impossible, stupid,* and *hopeless* are commonly used by someone who is thinking in extremes. On the other hand, words like *maybe, sometimes, once in the while, right now, mistake,* and *possible* are common words and phrases used by someone who is thinking in more flexible terms.

Remember that thoughts are not facts. You may have thousands of thoughts every single day, but that doesn't make them all true. This is where mindfulness comes in. It helps you to focus on the present so you are more aware of your thoughts and can turn the negatives into positives.

more to do

Now let's explore your thinking styles.

Zebra Thinking	You see things in black-and-white categories. It's all or nothing. If you don't get it just right, you see yourself as or feel like a total failure: *I can have all of the chocolate cake or none at all.*
End-of-the-World Thinking	You overestimate the importance of things: *I gained a few pounds, and I am so fat. No one will ever want to date me. I'll die alone.*
I Should or I Must	You attempt to motivate yourself with *should*, *shouldn't*, *must*, and *ought*. This often sets you up for guilt. If you don't follow the *should*, you feel like a bad person: *I shouldn't eat that. I know better.*
Fortune-telling	You predict that things will turn out badly. That prediction feels like an established fact: *I have trouble not eating the entire bag of chips. I know I'll do it.*
Mind-reading	You assume you know what other people are thinking, and generally it is negative. This is often just an indication of what you're thinking, not the other person: *She's looking at my plate; she must be thinking I am eating too much.*

journal exercise

During the upcoming week, write down any black-and-white statements that come into your head or pop out of your mouth. You may be amazed at how rigid your thinking is and how hard you've been on yourself. After you've written down the statements for a few days, go back to them and find a new way to phrase them—one that shows more flexible thinking. Over time, this new way of thinking will become routine.

- *I will never get into college with my terrible GPA!* can be rephrased as *I'm going to work really hard this year, and that will bump up my GPA!*

- *I slept in and was late for work; I'm hopeless when it comes to being on time!* can be revised as *I slept in today, so I'm going to make an effort to get to bed earlier and set two alarms on my phone.*

- *I ate so much food last night and haven't exercised for a week. I may as well just mail it in!* can be transformed into, *Today I am going for a hike, and I will be more mindful about the food I am eating.*

_____

_____

_____

_____

_____

_____

coping with perfectionism 27

Rachel: *I struggle with feeling not good enough. If I can't be the best at something, I don't want to do it at all.*

for you to know

You may excel at reading but really struggle with math. Singing may be your thing, but you've never really gotten the hang of dancing. You may have aced a math test on Monday, only to miss every other question on a quiz on Wednesday. Nobody is perfect, and that's what makes us human. Trying to be perfect only leads to one thing: anxiety. If you're feeling anxious about the things you struggle with, you may not be fully present to enjoy the things you excel at. Perfectionism is another part of black-and-white thinking. If it's not perfect—it's pointless. But this simply isn't true.

Think of it like this: If you've set a positive intention and done your best to follow through on it, you're doing things exactly as you're supposed to. Even if you can't achieve that intention perfectly—or sometimes, not at all—it doesn't mean you're a failure. Mistakes are a gift. Not only do they teach us and help us grow, but they also keep us humble. And that's an important quality to have. Humility helps you to be more compassionate toward yourself and others.

for you to do

First, take inventory of all your responsibilities and things that tug at your perfectionism (body image, grades, sports, and so forth). On this graphic, let's take a look at what you have on your plate. Divide the plate into sections, with the biggest section being what takes up most of your time and energy.

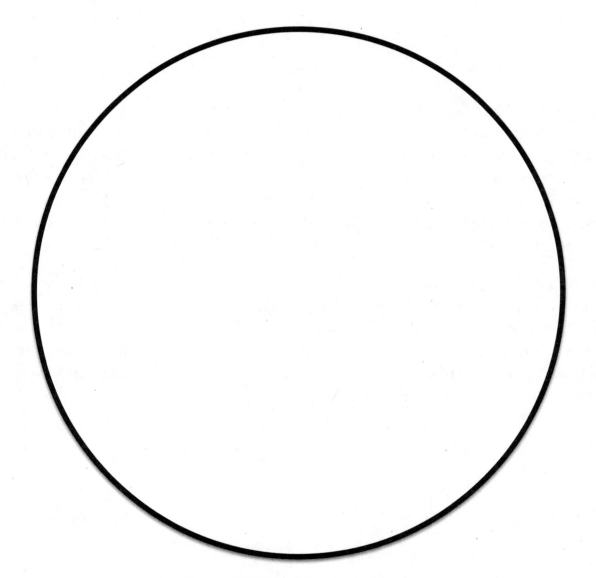

Figure 10. **What Is on Your Plate?**

Now, take one of the sections in your plate and figure out where you should set the bar for what you can achieve. When you set the bar too high, you always feel disappointed. Look at the figure and think about where you usually set your bar, and then how you can move it to a place that is achievable, realistic, and good enough.

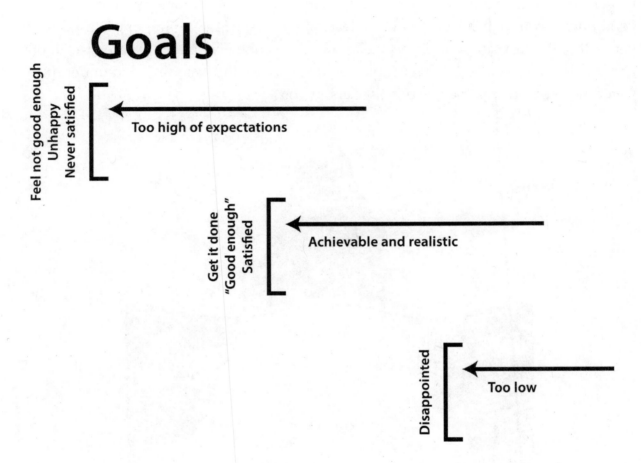

Figure 11. Perfectionist and Realistic Goals

more to do

We are invested in showing people a certain side of who we are. You may find yourself putting a smile on your face every day, when really you feel depressed. You are afraid to show people the real you. This is normal. Parents often encourage you to make a good impression, right? A problem can develop if you start hiding important aspects of yourself or if you're afraid to let people know who you really are. In this exercise, in the graphic below, write about what people see of you above the waterline, and under the waterline, write in what people don't see about you.

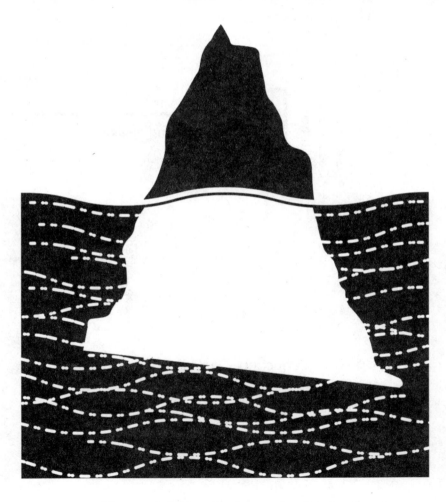

Figure 12. **What Is Below the Surface?**

Now take a look at what is under and above the surface and answer these questions.

Is there a certain image that I am trying to project to the world?

_____

_____

_____

_____

If people knew what was below the surface, I am afraid they would think…

_____

_____

_____

journal exercise

Journal about times when you've been a perfectionist or have set the bar so high that it was hard to reach. How did you feel during these times? How can you reframe these thoughts to change your feelings? Below are some prompts to help shape your thinking.

- I used to think: *If I can't* _____, *I'm going to…*

- But now I think: *Even if I can't achieve that goal, I'm going to…*

- The worst thing that can happen is…

- Will this matter in five years, five months, five weeks, or five minutes?

_____

_____

_____

_____

_____

_____

summary

Congratulations! You made it through the entire book. Give yourself a pat on the back, and do a little victory dance. You have learned a lot of great tools, and that's something you should be proud of.

Now it's time to make your Mindful Eating Pledge. On the next page, you will see a summary of what you've learned from this book. Agree to follow it as your new lifestyle. As a daily reminder, you can hang this pledge next to your mirror or by your desk. Use a highlighter to emphasize the statements that you want to remember the most. (You can download a copy of the pledge from http://www.eatingmindfully.com.)

However, please remember that nobody is perfect. Allow this Mindful Eating Pledge to be your guideline—rather than a set of rigid rules you enforce for yourself.

The Mindful Eating Pledge

I agree to eat mindfully.

I agree to keep myself hydrated.

I agree to boost my energy levels naturally.

I agree to get more quality sleep.

I agree to soothe myself without food when I am feeling emotionally hungry.

I agree not to let social media fool me into thinking that I'm fat or unattractive.

I agree to say no and stand my ground.

I agree to keep a positive mindset.

I agree to stop comparing myself with others.

I agree to stop chitchat about dieting with my friends.

I agree to listen to uplifting and motivating music when I feel down.

I agree to put away the scale.

I agree to be calm before making food decisions.

I agree to eat foods that help me focus and that boost my mood and energy.

I agree to use positive mantras when I need them.

I agree to let go of the past.

I agree to be grateful.

I agree to let go of black-and-white thinking.

I agree to ask for support when I need it.

I agree to stop trying to be perfect and accept myself as I am.

I agree to love my body exactly the way it is right now.

I agree to love myself exactly the way I am right now.

Sign: _____   Date: _____

Notes:

additional resources

Resources for Teens:

Find free bonus videos on how to cope with stress at www.eatingmindfully.com/teens.

Resources for Parents and Health Care Professionals:

Find free bonus videos on the best strategies for talking to your teen about food, stress, and boosting their confidence (without getting eye rolls or attitude) at www.eatingmindfully.com/parents.

Susan Albers, PsyD, is a *New York Times* bestselling author and licensed clinical psychologist at the Cleveland Clinic specializing in eating issues, weight loss, body image concerns, and mindfulness. She graduated from the University of Denver, completed an internship at the University of Notre Dame, and was a postdoctoral fellow at Stanford University. Her work has been quoted in *O, The Oprah Magazine*; *Family Circle*; *Self*; and *The Wall Street Journal*, and she conducts mindful eating workshops internationally. She was a guest expert on *The Today Show* and *The Dr. Oz Show*. Visit Albers online at www.eatingmindfully.com.

More ⏱ Instant Help Books for Teens

An Imprint of New Harbinger Publications

**THE PERFECTIONISM
WORKBOOK FOR TEENS**

Activities to Help You Reduce
Anxiety & Get Things Done

978-1626254541 / US $16.95

**THINK CONFIDENT,
BE CONFIDENT FOR TEENS**

A Cognitive Therapy Guide to
Overcoming Self-Doubt & Creating
Unshakable Self-Esteem

978-1-608821136 / US $16.95

**THE BODY IMAGE
WORKBOOK FOR TEENS**

Activities to Help Girls
Develop a Healthy Body Image in
an Image-Obsessed World

978-1626250185 / US $16.95

**THE TEEN GIRL'S
SURVIVAL GUIDE**

Ten Tips for Making Friends,
Avoiding Drama & Coping with
Social Stress

978-1626253063 / US $16.95

THE MINDFUL TEEN

Powerful Skills to Help You Handle
Stress One Moment at a Time

978-1626250802 / US $16.95

**THE ANXIETY WORKBOOK
FOR TEENS**

Activities to Help You Deal
With Anxiety & Worry

978-1572246034 / US $14.95